101 *Great* YOUTH SOCCER DRILLS

101 *Great* YOUTH SOCCER DRILLS

GREAT DRILLS AND SKILLS FOR BETTER FUNDAMENTAL PLAY

ROBERT KOGER

McGraw·Hill

New York   Chicago   San Francisco   Lisbon   London   Madrid   Mexico City
Milan   New Delhi   San Juan   Seoul   Singapore   Sydney   Toronto

Library of Congress Cataloging-in-Publication Data

Koger, Robert L.
    101 great youth soccer drills : great drills and skills for better fundamental play /
Robert L. Koger
        p.   cm.
    ISBN 0-07-144468-8
    1. Soccer for children—Training.   I. Title: One hundred one great youth soccer
drills.   II. Title: One hundred and one great youth soccer drills.   III. Title.

GV944.2.K64   2005
796.334'083—dc22   2005001362

7   8   9   10   11   12   13   DOC/DOC   1   5   4   3   2   1   0

ISBN 0-07-144468-8

McGraw-Hill books are available at special quantity discounts to use as premiums and
sales promotions, or for use in corporate training programs. For more information, please
write to the Director of Special Sales, Professional Publishing, McGraw-Hill, Two Penn
Plaza, New York, NY 10121-2298. Or contact your local bookstore.

This book is printed on acid-free paper.

Contents

Foreword

Coaching soccer begins with teaching individual players the basic techniques, or skills, they will need to deal with the ball under all of the various conditions that occur in a game. As we master our techniques through drills during our training sessions, we then move on to teaching our players tactics. We do this by starting with the smallest unit possible—1 player versus 1 player (1 vs. 1)—and gradually working up to the entire team situation—11 players versus 11 players (11 vs. 11). In *101 Great Youth Soccer Drills*, it is the players for game situations that the author has focused upon, and that is what makes it such a special coaching manual. There is a need for this type of literature in coaching soccer at the youth level.

Players have to become technically sound in soccer at a young age; once a player learns a technique, it takes countless hours of practice through training drills for this technique to become skill, which is the ability to use the technique to advantage during conditions and restrictions of a game.

As the U.S. Under-17 Men's National Team head coach, I use training drills every day to improve players' technical ability and their tactical awareness. Players such as Landon Donovan, DaMarcus Beasley, Bobby Convey, and Freddy Adu have spent many hours on the soccer fields in Bradenton, Florida, mastering technique and becoming better tactically in order to become successful international soccer stars. As a coach I am a big believer in practicing the same drill over and over again until that technique becomes skill and tactical awareness becomes instinct.

To me, teaching the game is the heart and soul of our sport. In all my years involved in coaching this sport, which has included high school, college, youth teams, amateur teams, and professional and national teams, I look back on my teaching time as the most rewarding. In the coaching profession it has always been the desire to create a resource to help the youth soccer coach in developing our young players technically and tactically by following a simple and organized plan. Robert Koger's drills will bring out the best in our youth players. They are challenging, competitive, and entertaining. The author delivers organized training drills that cover all the essential elements important to improving development in youth soccer players. While the game itself offers many opportunities for a young player to improve, it is still important for the coach to have a book that contains game-related drills, small-sided games, and basic coaching drills.

As a coach you have to plan that next training session. Whether it is preseason or postmatch, you must give some thought to utilizing the right drills that are appropriate to reach the desired result. *101 Great Youth Soccer Drills* is an excellent resource for helping the youth coaches find solutions to any problems they may encounter in the game. Bottom line is always the players and how the coach can make them better technically and tactically. Each drill has been diagrammed, showing the correct organization and identifying the objective and proper sequence.

All of us involved in this wonderful sport of soccer can enjoy watching a game at the highest level and having an appreciation for how the ball is played, the connection of a team through intricate passing, and the pure passion when a goal is scored, but there is always a beginning to this final product, and that is the countless hours spent on a field practicing as a young player with a coach running organized training drills with the objective of getting to the next level of play.

—John Ellinger, Head Coach
U.S. Under-17 Men's
National Team

Preface

A few years ago I was teaching a beginners coaching clinic. As I looked out at the group, I saw a man I knew had been coaching at least 10 years. I finished the clinic and walked over to the coach and asked him why he was there. He stated that his team was not winning and that now he knew why. He said that he had gotten away from the basics. This book prepares the beginning coach, assists and refreshes experienced coaches, and provides all the basic drills for coaching.

101 Great Youth Soccer Drills is the only "how-to" book you will ever need on soccer drills. With this book you can go from a beginner to an advanced coach. It is laid out in a sequence that allows any coach to become a master at teaching soccer. For those coaches who are new, it steps sequentially through the skills and the drills. For experienced coaches, each section is formatted to enable you to quickly find the information you need to conduct productive training. All information is easy to understand and is written to be used in a separate and stand-alone sequence. This allows you to teach what you need, when you need it.

This book completely covers the needed drills to prepare your players. It will become ragged with use. It is specifically designed to be used from the beginning of your journey as a coach to becoming the expert. No matter how experienced or inexperienced you are, you will not leave this book on the shelf once you have scanned the comprehensive contents and seen the easy-to-use format. This book is organized from the simple to the complex, using a building-block sequence. This allows you, the coach, to design your personalized training program by using drills to teach your players the game of soccer.

The information here is a result of more than 25 years of coaching youth soccer. Many of the drills and exercises are not original but have been picked up over the years and found to be the most effective in developing skills. There are many soccer books on the market, but very few take into consideration that you, the coach, do not have access to a wide array of equipment for training. Nor do you have an excessive amount of time. One book I read said to use a 50-foot-long wall, three feet high, and in another section it talked about the sandpit for goalkeeper training. These are not normally on the fields used to teach youth soccer. All of the equipment and field areas used for the drills in this book are easily available.

Coaching soccer *can* be fun. If you know what to do and your team is performing well, it is a lot of fun. If you don't know what you are doing and your team looks like an undertrained kickball team, fun is not a word you would use. This book provides the information that you need to start coaching and produce a real soccer team, making soccer enjoyable for you and the players.

My soccer philosophy is that success is measured by a team that plays well together, has fun, and learns soccer and athletic skills. The greater the degree of each of these three components, the greater the odds your team will be a winning team. Soccer is a game that allows every child to have fun and be part of a team. Size, shape, and special talent are not the key factors. Teams range from playing for fun to highly competitive. Every child can find a place in soccer. You, the coach, must decide on the balance for your team and, more important, what kind of coach you want to be.

Remember, soccer is more than just another athletic sport. It is an opportunity for children to socialize in a safe, structured environment. It is a chance for families to enjoy activities together and give life-critical support to children developing confidence and a sense of identity. The more fun you make the game for the players and the more conducive you make the game for the whole family, the more successful you and your team will be. You are the most important aspect of youth soccer. You are the coach.

Acknowledgments

I would like to thank Editor Mark Weinstein, Editorial Team Leader Craig Bolt, and the staff at McGraw-Hill for giving me this opportunity. Mark and Craig are the ideal editors. They know what is needed and are straight and to the point. They are a real asset for an author. I would also like to thank the dynamic duo of literary agents, Chamein Canton and Eric Smith of the Canton Smith Literary Agency. They took a chance on a beginning writer and worked hard to get my book published.

Another big thank-you has to go to my children, Denise, Jay, and Tony. They allowed me to be their coach and let me spend time with them. Last but certainly not least is my wife, Mary. She is my most ardent fan and strictest critic. Many games she would come down out of the stands and whisper sweet nothings in my ear, such as, "Your left halfback isn't overlapping," or "The other team's right fullback always moves to the right and clears with the right foot." She supported me with the practices and games as well as the book. She reviews everything, and without her this book would not have been possible.

1

Beginning a Practice—Warming Up and Stretching

It is essential to have a practice that supports and prepares the development of the players. Performing drills that enhance the players' skills is a must, but there is no shortcut to success. Your players must build strengths needed for the game. The drills in this book are all designed not only to teach the skills but also to develop cardiac endurance and strength.

Teaching the basics through the use of drills in practice must be done as a stair-step process. Every practice must start with warm-up and stretch, progress into the teaching of technique training and drills, and then move into drills that teach game tactics. This chapter addresses how to run a practice and then focuses on the first step in that process.

Ingredients of a Good Practice

* **Warm-up and stretching** activities enable the players to stretch their muscles, develop needed muscles, and get ready for practice.

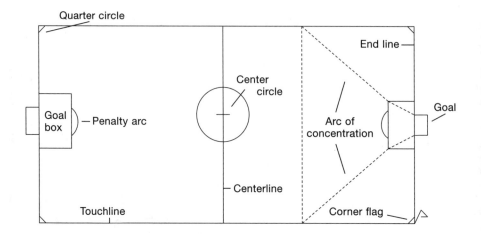

Figure 1.1 **Soccer Field**

- **Technique training/drills** help players develop skills necessary to play soccer.
- **Teaching tactics** allows players to learn how to play in formation, move to open space, etc.

Overall Practice Objectives

Each practice must have a specific objective. Concentrate on one or two skills per week. Make a practice schedule that covers different drills per week. Once you have started playing the games, do the drills required to highlight the skills that you notice your team is lacking during game play.

Fitness is a must. Many games are won at the end when the other team wears out. Make sure your fitness activities are drills that include the soccer ball as much as you can. Don't just run the players; have them work with and dribble the ball during all of your activities.

Fitness Categories

- **Cardiovascular endurance.** Building endurance is necessary to fully compete.
- **Muscular strength.** Soccer builds different muscular strength from what is required in other sports, and you must focus on what is needed for soccer.

Outcome of Fitness

- **Endurance** allows for long-term play in practices, games, and multigame tournaments.
- **Mind control** is necessary to be able to think under the stress of running, getting bumped, etc. Controlling the mind is a must to control the body through fitness.
- **Agility** allows players to be able to move with balance.
- **Strength** lets players jump, run, and move quickly.
- **Quick reaction time** is helpful to think quickly and then execute the desired move.
- **Speed and quickness** are required to execute the skills needed for offense and defense.
- **Coordination** is important to stay on the ball, see other players, and execute plays.

When you set up the teams, or groups, to compete against each other, use Team A or B, not 1 or 2. Children learn early that it is important to be number one, and they feel put down, or not worthy, if they are number two.

Note: Make sure each player brings a ball to practice.

Warm-Up and Stretch

Slow Running Drills

Running in Formation

I find that running in formation is a good way to build teamwork. This gives the players the opportunity to learn how to stay in step by following your guidance and count. It is also impressive to have your team run around the field, prior to playing the game, in perfect formation. The opposing team will see this, and you will have a slight edge.

Preparation: This uses the whole team.

Execution: Have all members of the team run, two abreast, staying in step. Cadence and actions should be called by yourself for the younger teams and by the goalkeeper for the older teams. This can be done by

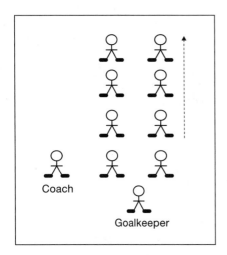

Figure 1.2 Running in Formation

saying, "left, left, left, right, left," as the players' feet hit the ground.

After the team has learned to run in formation, you can easily add aspects that enhance the warm-up run, teach soccer skills, and make it fun. While the team is running in formation, you or the goalkeeper (last person in the formation) should yell things like, "header." On the next step, all players jump up and do a header movement. Others are, "high step" (lifting the knees high while running), "side step" (running sideways, making sure the players' legs never cross over each other), and "hand touch" (touching the ground with the right or left hand). You can use anything that incorporates soccer skills. Sometimes the players will have some of their own they may want to do. This makes the running more interesting and contributes to the warm-up of the players.

Follow the Leader

This develops players' ability to follow orders and to dribble with their heads up, watching other players.

Preparation: This uses the whole team, each player with a ball.

Execution: Have one person start dribbling, and have all of the other players follow the person in front of them, staying in a single-file line.

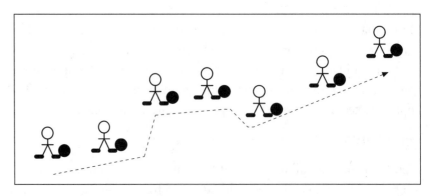

Figure 1.3 Follow the Leader

The lead player makes numerous moves, and each player must imitate those moves. The leader can dribble, jump, roll, do a somersault, etc. The players who follow must dribble the ball and do the same things the leader does. Pick out an outgoing player or use the assistant coach to lead the pack. As the coach, you must watch and correct the dribbling, jumping, etc.

Roll Over

Control of the ball, often referred to as "touch on the ball," is a necessity in soccer. This drill is fun, and the more the players do it, the better their control of the ball. The players may be awkward at first and may have trouble keeping the ball moving and going in a straight line. That will disappear as they become more proficient. This develops touch on the ball, balance, and agility.

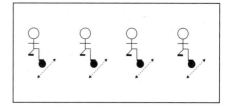

Figure 1.4 Roll Over

Preparation: This drill requires each player to have his own ball.

Execution: Have the player place the ball on the ground, to his right side. Then have him roll the ball straight down the field (in the direction he is facing) by pointing his right foot sideways and rolling it over the top of the ball (from back to front). This needs to be continuous movement. Do not let the player stop running while rolling the ball with his foot. Emphasize going straight for 20 or more yards. When the player reaches the distance you have established, have him return down the field using his left foot.

Karaoke

This drill covers just about everything you want a soccer player to do. It may be difficult for the player at first, but it becomes easy as it is repeated. All soccer players must learn to run, handle the ball, and keep their balance. This drill is the granddaddy of all drills to develop those skills. This is great for teaching agility, balance, touch, and movement of the ball and for building cardiac endurance.

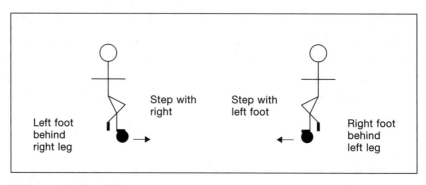

Figure 1.5 Karaoke

Preparation: This drill requires each player to have her own ball.

Execution: Walk the player through the routine prior to actual practice. Have the player place the ball in front and just outside of her left foot. Then have the player place her right foot so her heel is even with the middle of the ball, on the back side of the ball. Using her right foot, she should go behind the left leg and tap the ball with the instep of the right foot, causing the ball to roll forward. The left foot should not move. After the maneuver is completed, reverse the action and kick with the left foot. Have the player place the ball in front and just outside of the right foot. Then have the player place her left foot so her heel is even with the middle of the ball, on the back side of the ball. Using her left foot, she should go behind the right leg and tap the ball with the instep of the left foot, causing the ball to roll forward. The right foot should not move.

Have all the players walk through this using both feet. When they have the concept down, have them slowly move down the field doing the maneuver by switching feet every other touch (left-right-left, etc.). As they improve their skill, pick up the speed until they have a fluid movement. Speed is not a requirement, but constant fluid motion is.

Stretching
After performing slow running drills to warm up, stretching is the next exercise. Have the players stand in a circle, and either you or your captain(s) stand in the center and direct the stretching exercises.

Reaching Out

Execution: Have the players stand with their legs apart and direct them left, right, and center. Have them go to the left and touch their toes (hold the position; this is static only, no bouncing). If players cannot touch their toes, have them bend as far as they can. Repeat this to the right and then the center. When stretching to the center, have the players reach down and back, in between their legs, as close to the ground as they can.

Figure 1.6 Reaching Out

Lift Legs Up Behind

Execution: Have each player stand straight up and then fold his right leg up behind him and hold it. The knee will be pointing directly toward the ground. The player will press the heel of his foot against his rear end with his hands, while standing on one foot. Repeat with left leg. Any time a player is standing on one foot, have him

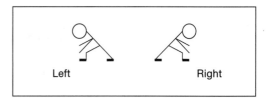

Figure 1.7 Lift Legs Up Behind

concentrate on an area four or five feet in front of him. If he looks straight down, he will have trouble keeping his balance.

Lean into Legs

Execution: Have the players stand with their legs apart. Then have them turn toward the right or left, keeping their legs apart with their feet pointing in the direction they are facing. Then have them lean forward placing their stomach against the top of the forward leg, which is bent. The back leg will be stretched out straight with that foot pointing toward the direction they are leaning.

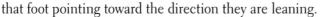

Figure 1.8 Lean into Legs

Toe Taps, Alternating Feet

Preparation: This drill requires that each player have a ball.

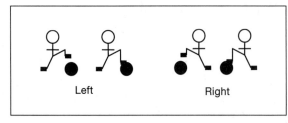

Left   Right

Figure 1.9 **Toe Taps, Alternating Feet**

Execution: Have the players put the ball in front of them. Using alternate feet (right then left), have them lift one foot at a time and place the sole of the tip of their shoe on the ball. Have them start slowly by just touching the ball, and as they develop their balance, pick up the speed until there is constant movement. Make sure they do not slap the ball with their feet, just tap it lightly. This develops balance, coordination, agility, and touch and is a good cardiovascular drill.

Touch Ball with Knee

Preparation: This drill requires that each player have a ball.

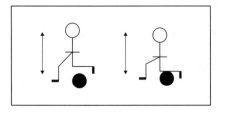

Figure 1.10 **Touch Ball with Knee**

Execution: Have the players put the ball to their right or left side (all do the same) so it is against their foot. Then have them lift the leg that is closest to the ball behind them and hold it with their hands. Then players will go straight down on one leg and touch the ball with their knee. After touching the ball, have the players lift themselves back up. Start with five or fewer touches and build as the players' strength builds. Do this with both legs.

Jump over Ball

Preparation: This drill requires that each player have a ball.

Figure 1.11 **Jump over Ball**

Execution: Have the players put the ball to their right or left side (all do the same) so it is against their foot. Have them keep their feet together and jump sideways over the ball, making sure that they don't spread their legs. Do this left, right, forward, and backward. Note that when you start this, some of the players may land on the ball and fall. This drill is good for the cardiovascular system, and it builds leg strength and heading ability.

Back to Back

Preparation: This drill requires one ball for every two players.

Execution: Have pairs of players stand with their backs to each other. Give a ball to one of the players, and have her lift the ball up over her head while the other player lifts his hands to take the ball. The player with the ball hands the ball to the other player, who then takes the ball, bends over, and passes it to the other player between the legs. Keep this action moving as steadily and as quickly as possible while maintaining control. This allows the players to stretch all of the muscles while working together.

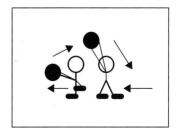

Figure 1.12 Back to Back

Other Warm-Up Exercises for Under-6 and Under-8

Crab Crawl

Execution: Get the players on their hands and feet in a four-point stance facing down or facing up, and have them crawl in this position. This is fun and stretches the arms, legs, back, and stomach muscles.

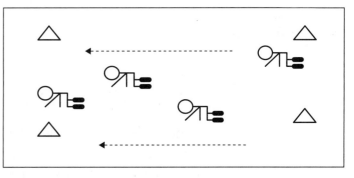

Figure 1.13 Crab Crawl

Touch Ball

Preparation: This drill requires that each player have a ball.

Execution: Have the players place the ball in front of them. Call out a part of the body that the players should use to touch the ball. You can call out "forehead," "elbow," "foot," etc. This gets the players to bend and stretch their arms, legs, back, and stomach muscles.

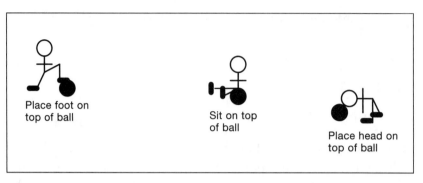

Place foot on top of ball

Sit on top of ball

Place head on top of ball

***Figure 1.14* Touch Ball**

Jump Rope

Preparation: This drill requires a long jump rope and a ball.

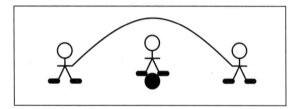

***Figure 1.15* Jump Rope**

Execution: Have two players twirl the rope and one player stand in a position to jump rope. The jumper places the ball between his feet and jumps while keeping the ball in place. This provides cardiovascular endurance, leg strength, and a sense of timing.

Line Jump

Preparation: This drill requires numerous cones.

Execution: Place cones in a straight line about three to five feet apart. Have players run and jump over the cones. After they finish, they can rest while they walk back to the starting point. After the players get in

***Figure 1.16* Line Jump**

better shape, work for continuous movement. Place the cones in a circle, and have players run and jump until you blow the whistle for them to stop. This provides cardiovascular endurance and leg strength.

Animal

Preparation: This drill requires four cones and a ball for each player.

Execution: Have players place the ball in front of them. Then have them get on their hands and knees. Set up two cones for a start area and two for a stop area (about 10 yards apart), and have the players push the ball with their head, having a race. As they get better, change to having them stand on their hands and feet (just hands and feet touching the ground, no knees touching) and roll the soccer ball with their head. You can make this any animal you want. You can have them be an elephant (using their nose), or a dog (using their head), etc. This builds leg and arm strength and limited cardiovascular endurance.

    Note: To prevent dehydration, you must have constant water breaks. You will not be running as much as the players will be, so keep a close watch on them.

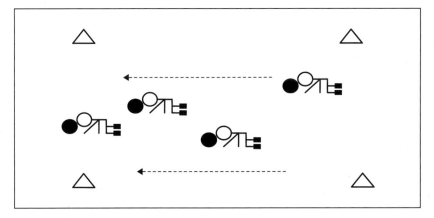

Figure 1.17 **Animal**

2

Teaching Techniques and Skills

Technique Types

There are three types of techniques that must be taught. Different people call them by different names. I use "FIG" because it is something I can easily remember. Here are the definitions for "FIG."

- **Foundation (F).** These techniques are the lowest level of training. They are used to develop the basic soccer skills needed by each player but do not get into actual game conditions. Building a strong foundation is necessary. As with building a house, the stronger the foundation, the bigger and more varied the house can be. These foundation skills are a must for every player.

- **Intermediate (I).** These are intermediate or midlevel techniques that are necessary to tie the foundation skills to the game skills. These are not the actual game skills but are used as building blocks to develop the actual game skills.

- **Game (G).** These are the actual skills needed for playing the game. These teach the players to be able to conduct themselves during games.

Note: The letters *F, I,* and *G* will be used in the drills to identify the skill level that is being taught.

Teaching

Teaching soccer techniques/skills is no different from teaching any other psychomotor skills. Use the demonstration-performance method following a simple teaching format: introduction, body, and conclusion. Tell players what you are going to teach them, demonstrate the technique/skill, and then have them perform. To learn, one must be told how to, be shown how to, and then practice how to. A suggested easy-to-use format follows. Remember, the younger the player, the shorter the attention span. Don't spend a lot of time lecturing.

- **Introduction.** Introduce the technique/skill to be taught and tell players why they are doing it and how it can help them learn soccer.
- **The Basics**
  1. Explain how the technique/skill works.
  2. Demonstrate the technique/skill you want the players to do.
  3. Have the players practice the technique/skill. While they are practicing, use general comments to get them to do the technique/skill correctly. These can be as simple as, "Keep moving; do not stop," or as complex as, "Roll your foot over the ball with the toe of your foot. Do not kick it." During the practice, walk among the players and give them specific corrections while still encouraging them. This can be done by saying things like, "That's pretty good, but if you do [whatever], it will be easier." When they do it correctly, you can then say, "Yes, that was perfect," or "Great job," and call them by name.
- **The Drills.** Run as many repetitions as is necessary to learn the technique/skill.
- **Conclusion.** Tell players how they did and make any overall corrections that are required.

3

General Practice Skills and Technique Drills—U-6/U-8

This chapter is made up of general practice drills designed for younger—Under-6 (U-6) and Under-8 (U-8)—players. Remember that all children like to have fun, and the more fun you make it, the happier they will be and the more eager to learn soccer.

Each of the drills in this section is set up so they can stand alone—you do not have to follow the sequence of the book. Go with the order of skills and techniques you want your team to learn. These are general practice drills and do not include the teaching of the skill. After the drill has been taught, these drills can be used to add fun to the practice. Each drill explanation includes a statement of what the drill accomplishes.

General Practice Drills—U-6/U-8

Snapping Turtle (F)

Have half of the team lie on the ground and use their arms to be the "snappers" while the other half, each with a ball, try to dribble through

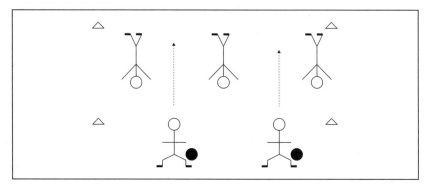

Figure 3.1 **Snapping Turtle**

them without the ball being "snapped" up by the other players' arms. Lay out cones to limit the area. Also tell the players on the ground that they can move only as far as they can reach. They cannot crawl or jump at the other players. Make sure there is room between the "turtles" for the players to dribble. After the players have run the turtle field four or five times, switch the players and repeat. This teaches the players to dribble and control the ball and also to move to open space (away from other players).

Somersault (F)

Line up all of the players, each with a ball, and have them start to dribble. When you blow the whistle, have them stop the ball, do a somersault, and then get the ball and continue dribbling. This develops

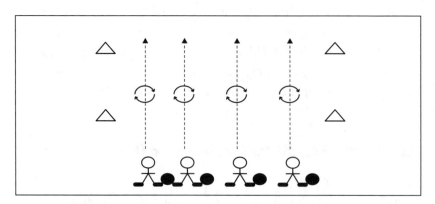

Figure 3.2 **Somersault**

cardiovascular endurance, teaches dribbling and picking up the ball, and stretches the players while they have fun.

Leapfrog (F)

Put half the team in pairs—two in a row, one in front of the other, about three to five yards apart. Have those players get on the ground on their hands and knees. Give a ball to players on the other half of the team. Have the players with the ball dribble up to those on the ground, pass the ball past the person on the ground to their left or right, leapfrog (jump) over the player on the ground, run to the ball that they passed, and continue dribbling toward the next player where they again pass the ball and leapfrog over them. After the players have leapfrogged the other players four or five times, switch the players and repeat. This teaches dribbling and passing and stretches players.

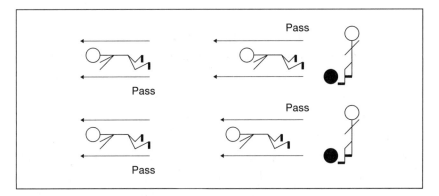

Figure 3.3 Leapfrog

Pass Through Goal (I)

Have half of the players stand in a line with their legs apart (their legs are a goal), side by side, with about two yards between players (goals). Place a cone five yards in front of and five yards behind each standing player (goal). Have the other players start at the cone in front of one of the standing players, dribble up to the player that is standing, and pass the ball through their legs. The players then move around the "goal," move to the ball, dribble the ball around the cone, and repeat. After the players have shot on goal four or five times, switch the positions of the players and repeat. This teaches dribbling, shooting, and ball control and builds cardiovascular endurance.

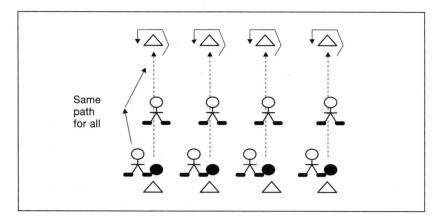

Figure 3.4 Pass Through Goal

Tag (I)

Line up all of your players and give them each a ball. Make one player "it." Have the player that is "it," or the tagger, count to 10. While that player counts, the others start dribbling wherever they want. The tagger must then run and tag each player as they dribble. After all players are tagged, change the tagger and go through this until everyone has been "it." You may want to put out cones that limit how far the players can go. Most will dribble slow, or in a small area. Some will go in a straight line and quickly get out of a decent range. This provides cardiovascular endurance and dribbling skills and enables the player doing the tagging to make choices.

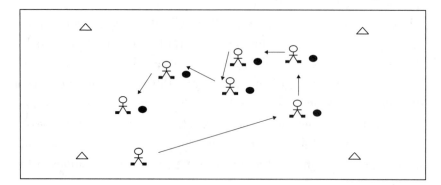

Figure 3.5 Tag

4

Passing and Kicking Instruction and Drills

Passing the soccer ball is how you get the ball from yourself to another player. You do this by kicking the ball. Kicking with accuracy is necessary in passing and scoring.

Note: When kicking the ball toward the goal, do not kick directly to the goalie. *Teach this from the beginning.* Place two or three cones in the right and left corners of the goal, and have the players shoot at the cones. The players will have a tendency to see the goalie and kick directly to the goalie. The goalie is the danger area, and all kicks must be away from the goalie (to the right or to the left).

The Basics

1. You must pass/kick the ball to the feet of the other player. If the pass is not accurate, the other team's players can get the ball.
2. Your body should be balanced over the ball with the knee pointing downward toward the ball.
3. Plant your foot next to the ball, with that foot pointing in the direction of the pass/kick you are going to make.
4. Hold the ankle of the foot passing/kicking the ball rigid, and let your foot and leg follow through on the kick.

Note: All players have a "sweet spot" on their foot—that place that will give them uniform and accurate kicks. It's located on the laces of the shoe, although the exact location varies by a small amount from player to player.

To help your players find their sweet spot, have them sit on the ground with their feet in front of them about 6 to 12 inches out from their body. They should be sitting comfortably and able to raise their foot, knee, and leg straight up. Then have them hold a ball above their head, drop it straight down toward the laces of their shoe, and raise their foot until it meets the ball. When they hit the sweet spot on their foot, the ball will go back up without any spin or rotation. If they hit the ball too high on the laces, it will spin away from them. If the ball is hit below the sweet spot, it will come back toward them. Hitting to either side of the sweet spot will cause the ball to go right or left away from them.

They should repeat this action until they are able to strike the ball and cause it to go straight up and straight back down without any spin or rotation. Mark this spot on the shoe using chalk or adhesive tape. Do drills using that marked spot on the shoe so the players can get used to hitting on the sweet spot.

Do not let players kick with their toe. If the kick is with the toe and happens be kicked perfectly, it will go straight. If the kick is to the right of center of the toe, the ball will go right; if it is left of center, the ball will be propelled left. Players cannot kick accurately by using the toe.

Passing/Kicking Drills

Soccer Golf (F)

Preparation: This drill requires cones and a ball for each player.

Execution: Place plastic cones around the field at different distances. Tell the players where to start and which cone is number 1, 2, 3, 4, etc. The players then kick the ball at the cone (hole) until the cone is hit. Have only one player, per hole, at a time. Concentrate on accuracy. Every time the player kicks the ball counts as one stroke. Players keep their own score, and the person with the lowest score wins. For Under-8 players, if someone scores a hole in one (hits the cone on one kick), yell out his name and tell him how good that was; this compels the others to try harder. This drill teaches accuracy, touch on the ball, and distance and is a fun game.

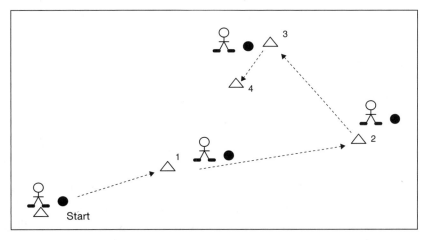

Figure 4.1 **Soccer Golf**

Knock Down (F)

Preparation: This drill requires cones and one ball for every two players.

Execution: Place cones in two parallel rows with a player behind each. The players behind one line of cones make up Team A; the players behind the other line of cones are Team B. The distance between the cones can be close or far (start close and then increase the distance as

Figure 4.2 **Knock Down**

the players improve). Have Team A kick to the opposite line of cones first and see how many they knock down, and then have Team B kick to their opposite line. Leave the knocked cones down. The team to knock all of the cones down first wins. This teaches accuracy and proper passing techniques.

Through Goal (I)

Preparation: This drill requires cones and one ball for every two players.

Execution: Set up two cones as a goal, approximately three feet apart, and have one player stand on each side of the cones, facing the opening of the cones (goal). The players then pass the ball to each other by putting it between the cones. Vary the distance of the players to the cones, starting short and increasing the distance as they improve. This teaches accuracy and also teaches the receiving player to move to the ball.

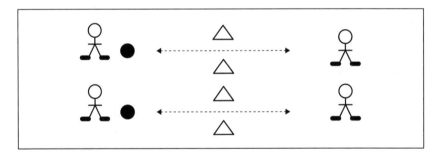

Figure 4.3 Through Goal

Throw and Kick (I)

Preparation: This drill requires cones and a ball for each player.

Execution: Set up two cones, three feet apart and approximately five to ten yards away, for each player; this is that player's goal. Have the player throw the ball over her head (forward or backward) and then run to the ball and shoot on goal. Also, have her throw it between her legs. Having a player throw the ball over her head backward requires her to turn toward the ball and quickly locate the ball, move to the ball, dribble, and then shoot. This teaches movement to the ball, dribbling, and passing/shooting.

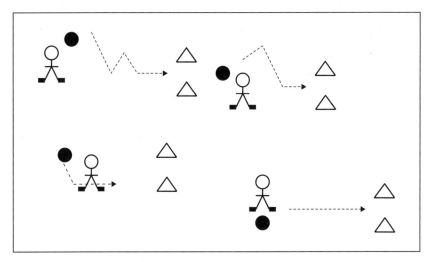

Figure 4.4 **Throw and Kick**

Through the Legs (I)

Preparation: This drill requires two or three soccer balls and a goal (can use cones to mark goal area).

Execution: Have players line up in a straight line, one behind another. Then have one player move out into the field, between you and the goal, with his back to the goal. The next step is for you to pass (kick) the ball, so it goes through the player's legs. Have the player turn and then move to the ball and either dribble to the goal and shoot, or shoot on goal using a one touch (kick only). You can direct one touch or dribble then kick. This teaches the players to pass, receive, and shoot.

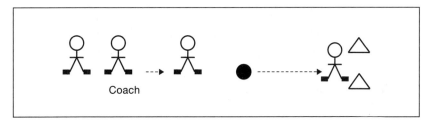

Figure 4.5 **Through the Legs**

Roll and Kick (G)

Preparation: This drill requires two or three balls and a goal (can use cones to mark goal area).

Execution: Have players line up in a straight line, one behind another. Give the first two or three players their own ball. Have the player at the front of the line pass the ball to the coach, who is standing between the line of players and the goal. The coach then deflects (passes) the ball to the right or left as the player moves to the ball. The player then shoots on goal. You can direct one touch (kick only) or dribble then kick. This teaches the players to pass, receive, and shoot.

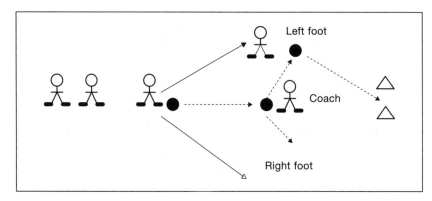

Figure 4.6 Roll and Kick

Water Balloon (F)

Preparation: This drill requires heavy-gauge balloons (one for each player plus a few spares) and cones.

Execution: Fill each balloon with water. Place the filled balloons on the ground, and have each player dribble a balloon without breaking it. Set up a start and finish line, using cones, and have the players compete against each other. Emphasize not breaking the balloons. Because the balloons will not roll easily, nor will they go straight, the players have to manage the balloons to get them where they need to go. This teaches the players proper dribbling technique and is fun.

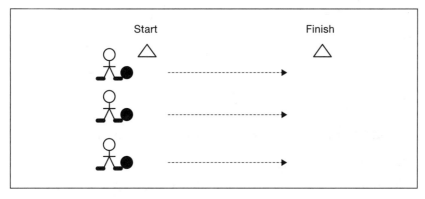

Figure 4.7 **Water Balloon**

Roll and Lift (I)

This will be very difficult for the Under-6 players, hard for the U-8s, and relatively easy for U-10s and above. Nevertheless, the kids like this drill, and it does develop great touch on the ball. Regardless of their age, let them try.

Preparation: This drill requires a ball for each player.

Execution: Have each player place a ball in front of himself close enough to put his foot on the top of the ball. Have the player place his foot on top of the ball and then roll the foot backward while keeping contact with the ball. This causes the ball to roll toward the player. The player then quickly places his foot on the ground directly in front of the ball as it rolls toward him. As the ball rolls up on his foot, the player lifts his foot and passes the ball down the field. The player must keep

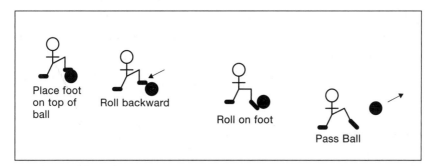

Figure 4.8 **Roll and Lift**

his ankle locked to do this drill. Let each player keep doing this until he can pass the ball straight. After this is taught, every time you ask the player to throw you the ball, have him use his feet rather than his hands.

Player Turn (I)

Preparation: This drill uses three players and two balls.

Execution: Put one player in the center, and the other two opposite each other, in front of and behind the center player. Have the center player turn her back to the outside person passing the ball. As the outside player passes the ball to the person in the center, he yells, "Turn." The player in the center turns, locates the ball, and passes (kicks) the ball directly back to the player that originally passed the ball. As soon as

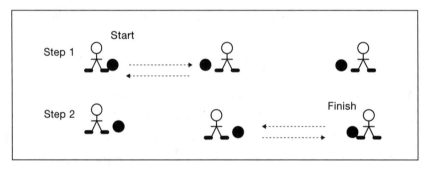

Figure 4.9 **Player Turn**

the center player passes the ball back, the other outside player passes the ball and yells, "Turn." This movement continues without stop. This requires the players to pass with both their right and left feet. Rotate players after 25 to 50 passes. This teaches the players to communicate on the field, quickly locate the ball, receive, and pass using both feet.

Weave (I)

Preparation: This uses three players, one ball, and a goal.

Execution: Have the three players line up on the centerline or end line with one player in the center and one player on each side. Make sure the players are at least five yards apart (can be farther). The center player (1) passes the ball to the front of the outside person and then runs behind that person, turns, and travels straight down the field. The player receiving the ball (2) dribbles to the center, and when reaching the center, passes to the front of the other outside person (3), running behind that person, turning, and going straight down the field. The player that received the ball (3) dribbles to the center and passes to the outside player (1). This continues all the way down the field. When in the area

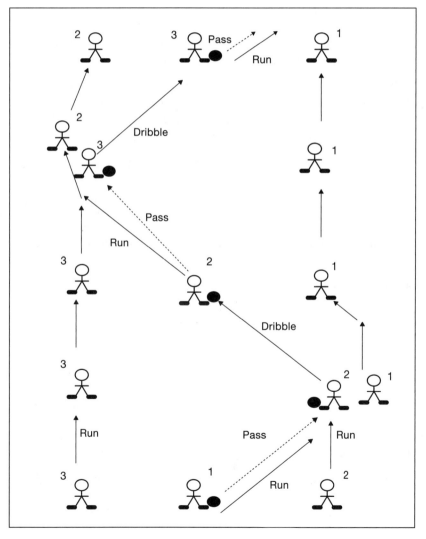

Figure 4.10 Weave

of the goal, whoever is on the outside and has the ball centers it while the other two shoot on goal. Make sure the players pass to the feet (while leading the player) and then go behind the person they passed to. This teaches them to lead their passes, cover the position of the player they passed to, dribble, center, and shoot on goal.

Wall Pass (G)

Preparation: This uses three or four players (two or three on offense and one on defense) and one ball.

Execution: Give one of the offensive players the ball. Have the defender facing and about five yards in front of the person with the ball. Put the other offensive player two or three yards away on the right- or left-hand side of the defender. The offensive player with the ball will dribble toward the defender but just before reaching him will pass the ball to the other offensive player, who is standing beside the defender. As soon as the player passes the ball, that player will go around the defender on the opposite side of the pass. The outside offensive player who just received the pass will redirect (pass) the ball behind the defender. The player who originally passed the ball then receives the pass and continues down the field. To add a challenge, you can add an offensive player on the other side of the defender so the defender will not know where the pass is going to go. This teaches distance judgment, passing, defense, and touch.

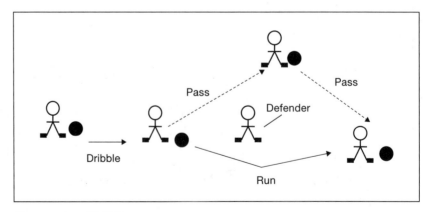

***Figure 4.11* Wall Pass**

5

Trapping and Receiving Instruction and Drills

Passing the soccer ball is imperative, but the person receiving the ball must be able to stop it or control it to complete the action. This is called receiving the ball. Trapping the ball is stopping the ball. You can receive the ball with your head, chest, thigh, or foot.

The Basics

1. When you see the ball coming, watch the ball, and move in front of it so you are ready to receive the ball.
2. Meet the ball with your foot, and then withdraw your foot (move your foot in the direction the ball was going) at contact to stop and retain the ball. If you stick your foot straight out and strike the ball, it will go away from you.
3. Control the ball on the ground with no bounce or roll away from you.
4. Move (dribble) to open space and play the ball to an open teammate as soon as possible.

Trapping/Receiving Drills

Throw-Receiving (F)

Preparation: This uses the coach (or player), one player to receive the ball, and one ball.

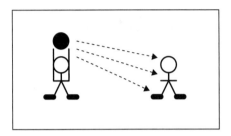

Figure 5.1 Throw-Receiving

Execution: The coach (or person throwing the ball) throws the ball to the player—to the chest, thigh, inside of foot, and head. No matter where the ball is thrown, the player moves that part of her body back upon contact to allow the ball to end its momentum and drop to a position where it can be played. Make sure the ball drops down and does not bounce out. This teaches receiving with all parts of the body.

Throw-Trapping (F)

Preparation: This uses the coach (or player), one player to receive the ball, and one ball.

Execution: The coach (or person throwing the ball) throws the ball in the air to the player or rolls it on the ground. No matter where the ball is thrown, the player moves to the ball and places his foot on the ball to stop (trap) it. When the ball is thrown in the air, have the player watch the ball very closely and place his foot on the ball just as it touches the ground, before it has a chance to bounce. This develops timing and coordination and teaches trapping with the feet.

Figure 5.2 Throw-Trapping

Kick and Collect (I)

Preparation: This drill requires one ball and all of the players.

Execution: Line all of the players on the centerline. The coach kicks the ball into the air (or rolls it on the ground). When the ball is kicked, the coach yells out the name of a player to receive the ball. That player moves to the ball and uses whatever proper technique (receiving or trapping) is required to capture the ball. The player then passes the ball back to the coach. (*Caution*: warn players not to use their head if the ball is kicked high in the air and has not touched the ground first.) This teaches players when to trap, when to receive, and to do so using the proper technique.

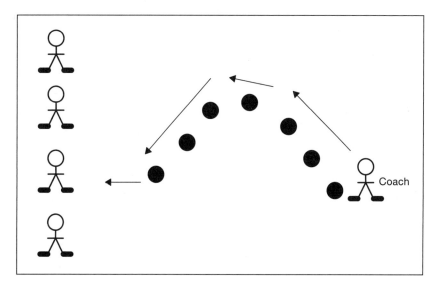

Figure 5.3 Kick and Collect

Kick and Return (I/G)

Preparation: This drill uses one ball, a goal, and all of the players.

Execution: This drill is the same as the Kick and Collect, but when the player collects the ball, that player will dribble to the goal and shoot. This allows the players to learn how to shoot on goal. You can introduce game techniques and increase the level of difficulty by having some of the players act as defenders. This teaches the players to trap/receive, play offense, play defense, dribble, and shoot using the proper techniques.

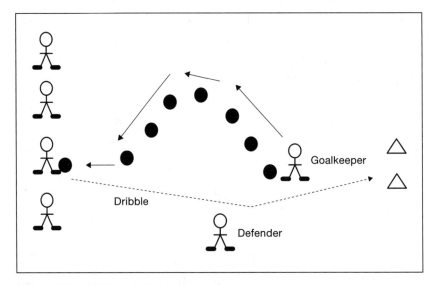

Figure 5.4 **Kick and Return**

6

Heading Instruction and Drills

Using your head is an effective way to redirect the ball when it is in the air. If this is done correctly, it will not hurt the player. Heading can be used to pass the ball to another player or to shoot on goal. When first teaching the players to head the ball, deflate the ball so it is soft. Also, be prepared to deal with bloodied noses.

The Basics

1. When the ball is coming, move so you are facing the ball and your body is directly in front of it.
2. Watch the ball all the way in, and continue watching the ball as it strikes your forehead.
3. Keep your eyes open—do not close them or you will get hurt—and watch the ball coming to you and going away from you.
4. Strike the ball with the upper-front portion of your forehead, not with your temples or the top of your head.
5. Move your head back and then forward to strike the ball; do not just stand still and let the ball hit you.

Heading Drills

All of these drills emphasize the movement involved in properly heading the ball. The players have to time their head movement with the arrival of the ball. The head must be moving forward as it strikes the ball.

Sitting and Knees (F)

Preparation: This uses two players and one ball.

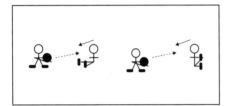

Figure 6.1 Sitting and Knees

Execution: Have one player sit on the ground with her feet straight out in front of her. Have the other player stand directly in front of her and throw the ball, underhanded, toward her. Make the throw short so the player heading the ball has to move forward to strike the ball. This teaches the player to move into the ball and not to let the ball strike her. Do the same with the player positioned with both knees on the ground. Again throw the ball short so the player has to lunge forward to strike the ball. The player can use her hands to keep herself from hitting the ground. This teaches proper techniques for using the head to direct the ball.

Head Out of Hands (F)

Preparation: This uses one ball for each player and cones.

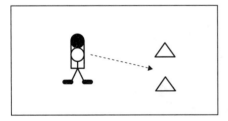

Figure 6.2 Head Out of Hands

Execution: To start, have players hold their own ball in their hands and knock the ball out of their hands by heading the ball. Do not let them move the ball to their head. They should move their head to the ball. Then set up cones and have the players head the ball to a specific location. This teaches proper heading techniques and accuracy for using the head to redirect the ball.

Heading While Standing (F)

Preparation: This uses two players and one ball.

Execution: Using the technique shown in Sitting and Knees, have one player throw the ball directly to the other player (not short). Have that player use the same head and body movement to head (pass) the ball back to the person that threw the ball. Make sure the person heading the ball moves his head back and is going forward when he strikes the ball. This teaches proper techniques for using the head to redirect the ball.

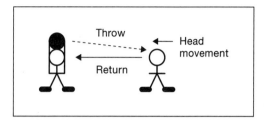

Figure 6.3 Heading While Standing

Heading with Three Players (I)

Preparation: This uses three players and one ball.

Execution: Place all three people in a triangle formation. Have the player that is going to head the ball facing the other two, with each of the other two slightly to the right and left of the player heading the ball. Have one person throw the ball, and have the header redirect it to the person who did not throw the ball. This will require the header to turn both her head and body to redirect the ball (the feet may not have to be moved). Make sure the header leans backward and strikes the ball while going forward. Alternate between the two throwers. After 15 to 25 headers, rotate the players. This teaches the players to properly head the ball and redirect it with accuracy.

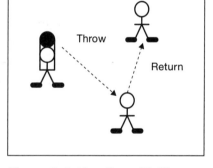

Figure 6.4 Heading with Three Players

Lift and Head (I)

Use this as your team has mastered the Roll and Lift, described in the passing drills area (Chapter 4).

Preparation: This requires numerous balls, two lines of players, a goal, and a goalkeeper.

Execution: Split the players into two groups, lined up on each side of the goal. Give one group the balls. The first member of this group then

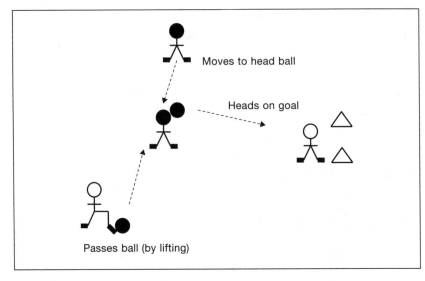

Moves to head ball

Heads on goal

Passes ball (by lifting)

***Figure 6.5* Lift and Head**

rolls and lifts a ball toward the center of the field (in front of goalkeeper). One player from the other side moves forward and heads the ball toward the goal. The goalkeeper tries to stop the ball from entering the goal. This teaches touch on the ball, teaches the players to run to the ball while adjusting to the location, and teaches them to head while on the move.

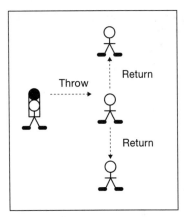

Throw

Return

Return

***Figure 6.6* Heading with Four Players**

Heading with Four Players (G)

Preparation: This uses four players and one ball.

Execution: The player heading the ball should face the person throwing the ball. The other players will stand to the right and left sides of the player heading the ball and facing toward that person. The thrower should throw the ball and have the player head the ball directly to one of the players on the right or left. This further amplifies the movement of the body and develops the timing to redirect the ball at a 90-degree angle.

Heading on Goal (G)

Preparation: This uses a goalie, a coach, and the team players.

Execution: With the goalie in the goal area, have a player start running toward the goal. Throw the ball into the air, and have the player adjust to the location of the throw by going to the ball. The approaching player then uses her head to direct the ball into the goal but away from the goalie. (This is another good time to teach the players that the goalie is the danger area.) She will be able to see the goalie and knows the goalie can grab the ball, so it is important that she direct the ball to the right or left of the goalie. Accuracy—as directing the ball to a small, specific area—is not important at this stage. Learning to place the ball away from the goalie is important. Be sure the ball is thrown at a distance far enough away from the goal to give the goalie a chance to play the ball. This teaches actual game heading, direction, and timing and allows the goalie to move and field (catch or knock away) live balls.

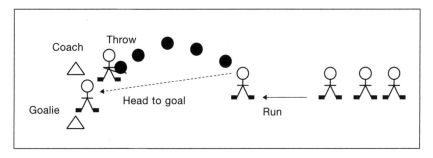

Figure 6.7 Heading on Goal

7

Shooting Instruction and Drills

Shooting the ball is necessary to score. If you can't shoot properly, you will not be able to compete in the game.

The Basics

1. When you shoot, do it quickly; do not hesitate or broadcast the shot. (In other words, don't stop the ball and back up to kick it, and don't dribble after you get it.)
2. Shoot the ball away from the goalie.
3. Put your weight into the kick and follow through with your leg.
4. Watch where you kicked the ball and move in the direction of the kick in anticipation of getting another shot.

   Note: Do not let your players kick with their toe. If the kick is with the toe and happens be kicked directly in the center, it will go straight. If the kick is to the right of center of the toe, the soccer ball will go right. If left of center, the ball will be propelled left. Players cannot kick accurately by using the toe.

Shooting Drills

Five-Ball Kick (F)

Preparation: This requires five balls, a goal, cones, a goalie, if desired, and the players split into two teams, A and B.

Execution: Place five cones in a straight line across the outer line of the penalty box (directly facing the goal) to indicate where the balls are to be placed. Facing the goal, if the players are kicking with their right foot, the balls should be on the left side of the cones. If using the left foot, the balls should be on the right side of the cones. Have Team A kicking and Team B gathering the balls to replace them. Place the balls so the player has to take a few steps in between kicks. Have each player on Team A, one at a time, kick all five balls toward the goal without stopping in between the kicks. Each ball that makes it into the goal is a point. After every player on Team A has kicked all of the balls right-footed, have Team B kick and Team A gather the balls. After Team B is finished, start over again with Team A using the opposite foot. The team scoring the most points is the winner. This teaches players to shoot on the move, develops a sense of goal location, requires them to shoot quickly, and teaches use of both feet.

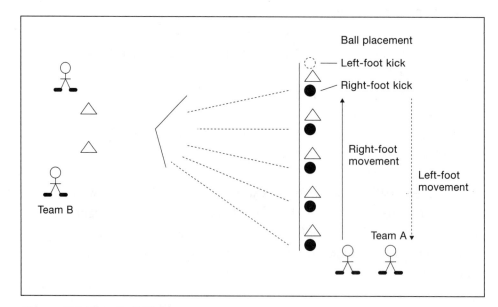

Figure 7.1 **Five-Ball Kick**

Nine-Ball Kick (F)

Preparation: This is the same as Five-Ball Kick but requires nine balls and a goalkeeper.

Execution: The difference is the placement of the balls. They go from one corner of the penalty box to the other. This requires the players to shoot at different angles and maintain their movement longer. Place nine cones across the entire outside line of the penalty box to indicate where the balls are to be placed. Facing the goal, if the players are kicking with their right foot, the balls should be on the left side of the cones. If using the left foot, the balls should be on the right side of the cones. Have Team A kicking and Team B gathering the balls to replace them.

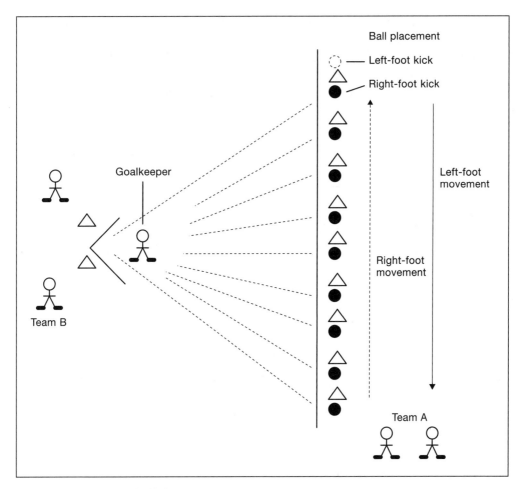

Figure 7.2 Nine-Ball Kick

Place the balls so the player has to take a few steps in between kicks. Have each player on Team A, one at a time, kick all nine balls toward the goal without stopping in between the kicks. Each ball that is within the left and right posts of the goal is a point. Have the goalie field the balls. After Team A has kicked all of the balls right-footed, have Team B kick and Team A gather the balls. After Team B is finished, start over again with Team A using the opposite foot. The team scoring the most points is the winner. This teaches players to shoot on the move, develops a sense of goal location, requires players to shoot quickly, teaches the use of both feet, and gives the goalie field practice.

Sit and Shoot (I)

Preparation: This uses one ball, one defensive player, the rest of the team, a goal, and a goalkeeper.

Execution: Have all of the players sit on the ground. Throw or roll the ball to a player, and have that player jump up, gain control of the ball, and shoot as quickly as he can. You can also place a defender between the sitting players and the goalie and place the goalie in the goal to field the ball. This teaches the players to shoot under any circumstances.

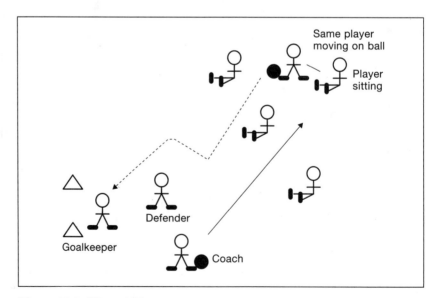

Figure 7.3 Sit and Shoot

Roll Ball (I)

Preparation: This requires numerous balls, a goalie, a goal, and the team.

Execution: Create four even groups of players. Place two of the groups, one on each side of the goal, standing by the goalpost. These players take the balls with them. Place the other two groups on the field, facing the goal and even with the goalposts. Have the front player that is in the right-side group on the field start running toward the goal. Have the front player that is in the group on the opposite side of the goalpost from the approaching player kick the ball toward the advancing player. That player shoots the ball into or toward the goal. Then have the other side do the same thing. Players retrieve the ball if they miss the goal and move in a counterclockwise position, assuming all four positions on the field. Keep the rotation moving at a fast pace. This teaches players to use whatever foot is appropriate, shoot on the run, and place the ball. The goalie receives field practice.

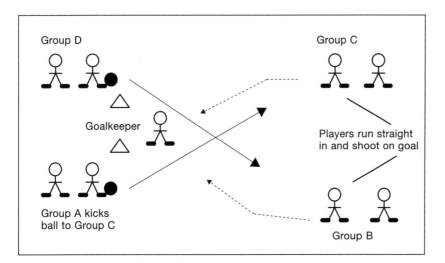

Figure 7.4 Roll Ball

Pass and Shoot (I)

Preparation: This requires two players, a ball, a goalie, and possibly a defender.

Execution: Place two players, one with the ball, on the centerline facing the goal. Have the players move toward the goal by passing the ball back and forth between them. As they approach the goal, they shoot (away from the goalie). This can be changed to a game-level situation by putting in a defender and requiring the players to time their passes to get a shot on goal. This reinforces dribbling, passing, and goal techniques and teaches shot timing.

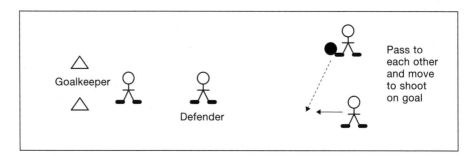

Figure 7.5 **Pass and Shoot**

Side-Ball Shoot (I)

Preparation: This requires a goalie, the entire team, two people (coach and assistant) to pass the balls, numerous balls, and cones for the goal.

Execution: Split the players into two groups. Line up one group so they are facing the right side of the goal and the other group facing the left side of the goal. Put the goalkeeper in the goal area. Position someone on each side of the players (coach and assistant) halfway between the players and the goal. Have a player from either side start moving toward the goal. Pass the ball to the player and have her shoot on goal. If she is coming from the left-hand side, the pass is from the right-hand side, and the player uses her left foot to kick on goal. Emphasize to the players that they need to shoot behind the goalkeeper. When the player from the right-hand side moves forward, pass from the left side, and have the player shoot with her right foot. Make sure your players switch lines each time. Some will want to stay in the same line so they can always kick with the foot they are the most comfortable with. Make them shoot with both feet. This drill teaches the players to judge the ball coming from the side, shoot at a point in the goal, and use both of their feet.

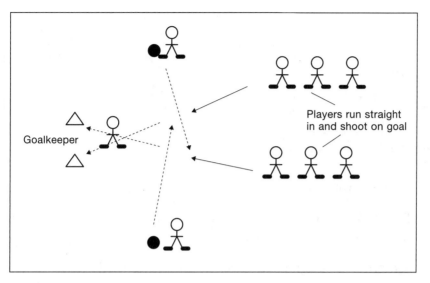

Figure 7.6 **Side-Ball Shoot**

Players run straight in and shoot on goal

Goalkeeper

Over-the-Head One vs. One (G)

Preparation: This requires a goalie, a defender, a thrower, and the rest of the team taking turns at the offensive role.

Execution: Have the offensive player turn with her back to the goal. Place the goalie and defender near the goal. Have the thrower throw the ball over the offensive player's head. At that time both the offensive and defensive players move to the ball. The offensive player should turn and go directly to the ball and make whatever moves are necessary to get around the defensive player to shoot. Quite often, the defensive player will win. As the players become more proficient, the offensive player will get off more shots. Remind players that they need to shoot when they get any opportunity, not wait for a perfect shot. After the shot or take-away, the offensive player then becomes defender and the previous defensive player gets back in line to become offense. This allows all players to play offense and defense and teaches shot timing, dribbling, and evasive actions. The goalie gets good field practice that is directly game related.

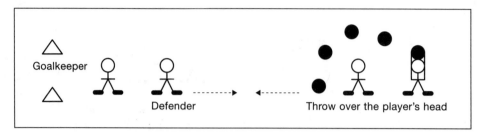

Figure 7.7 Over-the-Head One vs. One

Quick Shot (G)

Preparation: This requires two teams, two goalkeepers, cones to split the field into three areas, and one ball.

Execution: Set up the field so it is divided into thirds. Make the center area bigger than the two end areas. The center area is for dribbling and passing only. Each player can touch the ball only two times while in the center area. After two touches, players must pass to get rid of the ball. They can then receive the ball back, but only two touches at a time. When the ball goes into the end areas, it must be shot. The ball cannot be dribbled or passed. The end area size can be adjusted for the size of the players. The younger and smaller the players, the shorter the end areas should be. This teaches the players to pass quickly, pass to an open area for shooting, and shoot quickly.

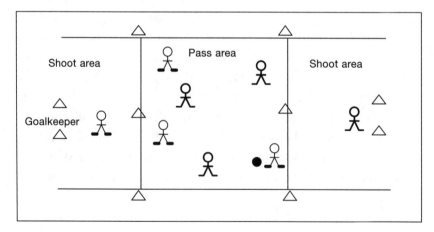

Figure 7.8 Quick Shot

8

Shielding Instruction and Drills

Shielding is a method used to keep the ball away from the defender while maintaining control. Shielding is used as an interim step only until you can move away from the defender or pass the ball to another teammate.

The Basics

1. Keep your head up and look for another person on your team to pass to, or dribble away from the opponent.
2. Keep the ball close to yourself so you can maintain control.
3. Position your body between the ball and the opponent.
4. Expect to be pushed by your opponent or be knocked off the ball. This is normal; keep your cool, and play on.

Shielding Drills

Roll Over (F)

Preparation: This uses one player and one ball.

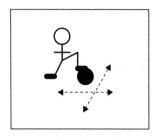

Figure 8.1 Roll Over

Execution: Have the player roll the ball by moving her foot over the top of the ball in the direction she wants the ball to go. The foot touches the ball gently and moves from back to front, front to back, right to left, or left to right depending on the direction the ball is to be moved. The player can move in circles, back and forth, or any direction. The player can also use her heel or toe. This teaches touch and ball control.

Donkey Tail (I)

Preparation: This uses cones, the entire team, one ball for each player, and enough old socks for each player to have one.

Execution: Using numerous cones, mark off an area that is large enough for all of the players to fit into but without a lot of excess room. Have all players put a sock in the back of their soccer shorts, hanging down like a tail. Players should not pull their shirt over the tail (sock), and they should position the sock so more than just a few inches of the sock sticks out. Put all of the players inside the area marked by the cones, and blow the whistle to start play. Each player has to dribble his own

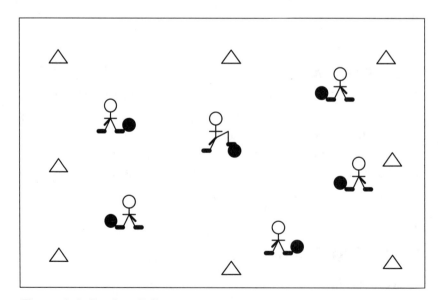

Figure 8.2 Donkey Tail

ball and maintain control while trying to pull the tail off of another player. If a player loses control of his ball and it goes out of the marked-off area, he must step outside the cones and wait until the next game to participate again. Each player that has his tail pulled must also step outside the cones. Have the players drop the tails on the ground when they remove one from another player. You will get down to just a couple of players who are left with their tails. As you get fewer and fewer players, you may want to decrease the size of the cone area. You can stop the drill when two players are left on the field. With just two players, it can go on forever. This teaches the players to shield and control the ball and to be aware of what is happening around them.

Two-Player Keep-Away (G)

Preparation: This requires two players and one ball.

Execution: Have the player with the ball continuously dribble and shield the ball while the defender tries to capture the ball. Change sides when the ball is captured by the defender. This teaches the offensive player to dribble and shield while the defensive player learns to capture the ball. Add additional players, and have two trying to get the ball away while two try to maintain control. This teaches the offensive players to get open, to pass, and to keep their head up to see the whole field. It teaches the defense to have patience, get the ball, and guard players to make interceptions. Overall, this drill teaches shielding and offense, defense, passing, and dribbling.

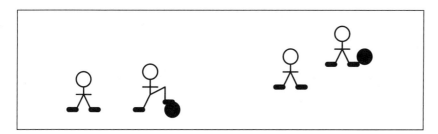

Figure 8.3 **Two-Player Keep-Away**

Karaoke (F)

Preparation: This drill requires each player to have her own ball.

Execution: This drill covers just about everything you want a soccer player to do. It may be difficult for the players to do at first, but it will become easier as it is repeated. Walk players through the routine prior to actual practice. They should begin by placing the ball even with and outside of their right foot; their weight should be on their right leg and foot. Then have them swing their left foot forward so that it goes behind the right leg and strike the ball with the instep of their left foot. The right foot should remain planted, or still, until the ball is hit with the left foot. As the ball rolls away, players move to the ball. Then they should hit the ball with the right foot: With the ball even with and outside of their left foot and their weight on the left leg and foot, they swing their right foot forward so it goes behind the left leg and strikes the ball with the instep of their right foot. The left foot should remain planted, or still, until the ball is hit with the right foot.

Have all the players walk through this using both feet. When they have the concept down, have them slowly move down the field doing the maneuver by switching feet every other touch (left-right-left, etc.). As they improve their skill, pick up the speed until they have a fluid movement. Speed is not a requirement, but constant fluid motion is. This is great for teaching agility, balance, touch, and movement of the ball.

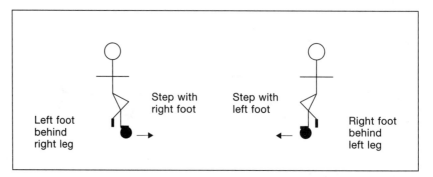

Figure 8.4 Karaoke

9

Dribbling Instruction and Drills

Dribbling is the method used to move the soccer ball from one place on the field to another with the feet. The ball must stay close to your feet so you can maintain control. It is very important to not continuously watch the soccer ball. You must keep your head up so you can see the field and your teammates.

The Basics

1. When dribbling, keep the ball as close to your feet as possible. Do not kick the ball and run to it.
2. Dribble with your head up. Do not focus on the ball.
3. When approaching your opponent, watch her hips and feet plant. This will tell you which direction to go. (If your opponent is facing left, go to his right so he has to turn to go with you; this gives you a few steps' head start. Also, if the player has one foot in front of the other, then dribble to the side of the advanced foot. Again, the person must reposition to catch up with you.)
4. Use fake movements—leaning right and going left, for example.

5. Vary your speed; keep your opponent off balance by slowing, speeding up, and cutting right and left.
6. Dribble away from your opponent; make her chase you. Always move to open space.
7. Look for another team member who is open so you can pass as quickly as possible.

Dribbling Drills

Follow the Leader (F)

Preparation: This uses the whole team, each with a ball.

Execution: Have one person start dribbling, and have all of the other players follow the person in front of them, staying in a single file. The lead player makes numerous moves, and each player must imitate those moves.

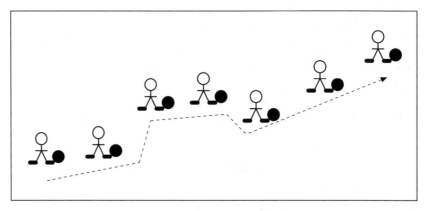

Figure 9.1 **Follow the Leader**

Home Base (F)

Preparation: This uses cones and the whole team.

Execution: Set up cones all over the field, and have players dribble to wherever they want. When the coach yells, "Home," the players must dribble to a cone as quickly as they can and then sit on their ball. Only one player can move to each cone. This teaches the players to dribble, observe players around them, and make decisions.

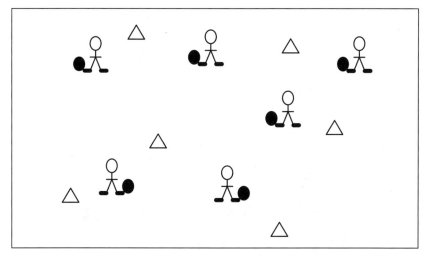

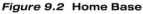

Figure 9.2 **Home Base**

Three-Player Keep-Away (I)

Preparation: This uses three players and one ball.

Execution: Have one person dribble while the other two try to take away the ball. Whoever gets the ball then dribbles while the other two try to get the ball. This teaches ball handling and vision.

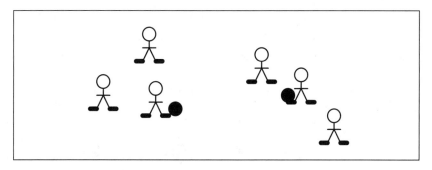

Figure 9.3 **Three-Player Keep-Away**

Hand in Air (I)

Preparation: This uses the whole team, each with a ball.

Execution: Have the players all dribble. The coach will hold one arm in the air with his hand holding up a number of fingers. When the coach yells, "Number," all players will have to continue dribbling while holding their arm in the air with the matching number. Do not let the players stop dribbling to see the number. This teaches the players to dribble while keeping their head up and watching something other than the ball or their feet.

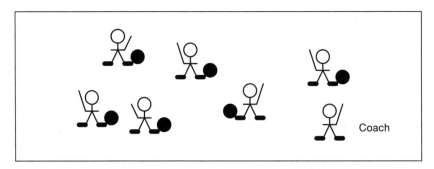

Figure 9.4 **Hand in Air**

Through the Cones (F)

Preparation: This uses the whole team, each player with a ball, and eight to ten cones.

Execution: Set up the cones in a straight row or staggered, and have the players dribble through them. Place the cones so the players have to move the ball in a straight line and also turn the ball. This can be done

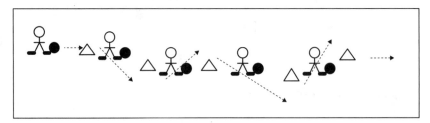

Figure 9.5 **Through the Cones**

with one player at a time, or you can split players into A and B teams and have them race across the entire length of the field with cones set at odd intervals to emphasize speed and control. This teaches the players to dribble, control the ball, and vary speed.

Donkey Tail (I)

Preparation: This uses cones, the entire team, one ball for each player, and enough old socks for each player to have one.

Execution: Using numerous cones, mark off an area that is large enough for all of the players to fit into but without a lot of excess room. Have all players put a sock in the back of their soccer shorts, hanging down like a tail. Players should not pull their shirt over the tail (sock), and they should position the sock so more than just a few inches of the sock sticks out. Put all of the players inside the area marked by the cones, and blow the whistle to start play. Each player has to dribble his own ball and maintain control while trying to pull the tail off of another player. If a player loses control of his ball and it goes out of the marked-off area, he must step outside the cones and wait until the next game to participate again. Each player that has his tail pulled must also step out-

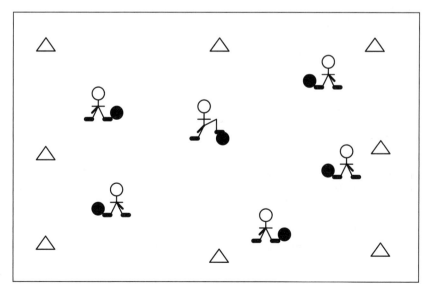

Figure 9.6 **Donkey Tail**

side the cones. Have the players drop the tails on the ground when they remove one from another player. You will get down to just a couple of players who are left with their tails. As you get fewer and fewer players, you may want to decrease the size of the cone area. You can stop the drill when two players are left on the field. With just two players, it can go on forever. This teaches the players to shield and control the ball and to be aware of what is happening around them.

Moving Goal (G)

Preparation: This requires three players and one ball.

Execution: Set up two people as offense and one as defense. Have the person with the ball dribble away from the defender while the other offensive player moves around the field and tries to get into a position that is open for a pass. When the player dribbling the ball has an opening, the player passes the ball to the other offensive player. That player must position herself so that the ball passes between her feet. Hence, her legs are the goal. The defensive player tries to stop the pass or take the ball away from the offensive players. This teaches offense and defense, ball control, dribbling, moving to the open, staying aware of the other players, shooting to the feet of your teammate during a pass, and receiving the ball by aligning with the pass.

Figure 9.7 Moving Goal

Three Goal (G)
This drill incorporates every skill and is perhaps the best drill to teach dribbling and passing.

Preparation: This drill uses the entire team (broken into A and B teams), one ball, and six cones.

Execution: Place the cones into three sets of two, each put in a triangle placement with about 10 to 20 yards between the pairs and about three feet between the two cones serving as the goals. Place the cones far enough apart so there is plenty of room to move and play soccer. The players can move anywhere on the field but cannot stand directly in front of any goal to block it. To start play, throw the ball in the air and let each team fight to get possession. Each team then moves the ball by dribbling, passing, etc., and they can shoot on any goal, from either side. However, after the ball passes through the goal, it must be touched first by one of their own teammates before it counts as a point. After each goal, restart play by throwing the ball into the air. To vary this drill, you can assign goalies to each team and let them use their hands, or you can make a rule that each player can touch the ball only one, two, or three times after the initial receipt. This drill incorporates every action a player uses in a game and teaches players to work together.

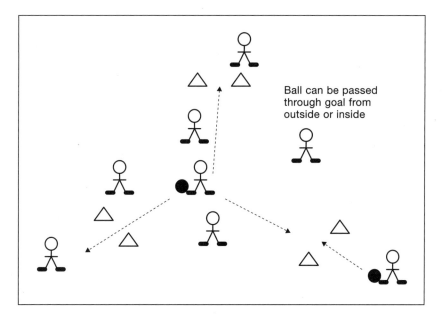

Ball can be passed through goal from outside or inside

Figure 9.8 **Three Goal**

10

Juggling Instruction and Drills

Juggling is not something that is normally done in a game. It is a method to teach control and touch on the ball and have fun while doing it.

The Basics

1. Drop the ball onto your foot (or thigh or head), and then pop the ball back into the air. Keep the ball moving up and down without using your hands.

2. When you are juggling the ball with your feet, thighs, or head, keep the ball at a constant level (low) while watching the ball closely. Do not hit it really hard and high into the air.

3. You can use your feet, thighs (just above the knee), or head to bounce the ball.

4. Set a goal of so many strikes, and try to reach it. Be sure to use your feet, thighs, and head. It is easier to use the knee, but the players need to use everything to control and juggle the ball.

Note: Start by having the players drop the ball to their feet or thighs and return it to their hands one touch at a time. This enables them to develop touch and control on the ball. It can be practiced by individuals at home.

Juggling Drills

Single Juggling (F)

Preparation: This uses the whole team, each player with a ball.

Figure 10.1 **Single Juggling**

Execution: Blow your whistle to have each player start to juggle the ball. No player can use the same areas (foot, thigh, or head) two times straight. The player who juggles the longest using feet, head, and thighs is the winner. Some players will be able to do this easily, while it will be more difficult for others. This teaches ball control and touch.

Team Juggling (F)

Preparation: This uses all of the players on the team broken into A and B teams with one ball for each group.

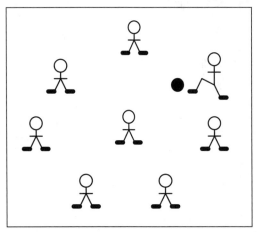

Figure 10.2 **Team Juggling**

Execution: Form the players into a circle with about three to five feet in between players. Place one person in the center of the group. Start play by throwing the ball to the center player. The center player kicks or heads (directs) the ball to one of the players in the circle. The player receiving the ball can move the ball to anyone. The team tries to keep the ball in play without allowing the ball to touch the ground. Two kicks is good to start but will increase as the team continues to do this drill. This drill is good when you want the players active but in a restful mode. This teaches control and teamwork.

Soccer Volleyball (I)

This is a drill I used as a reward for the players. We would go to the park and play volleyball using our feet and heads. A crowd normally gathered to watch the play. The players loved the game—and the attention.

Preparation: This requires two teams (A and B), one ball, and a tennis court or volleyball court with a net.

Execution: Place each team on opposite sides of the net. Have one player serve the ball over the net (using his hands to drop the ball to his feet for the serve) to the opposing team. Each player can strike the ball only once and can use everything except the hands. The game is identical to volleyball but uses a soccer ball and the players use their soccer

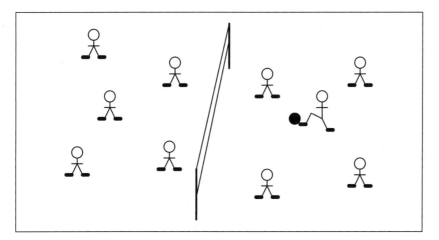

Figure 10.3 **Soccer Volleyball**

skills. This is a fun activity that allows your players to learn and relax at the same time. You can also add a goalie on each side who can use his hands to strike the ball. This teaches control, direction, and teamwork.

11

Throw-In Instruction and Drills

Throw-ins are how play is restarted after the ball goes out of play by passing over the touchline. Proper throwing of the soccer ball can be a real advantage to a team by allowing the team to maintain possession of the ball.

Some players will see a throw-in where the player runs forward, places the ball on the ground with her arms straight out, tumbles over to her feet, and throws the ball. This is done to get better distance. *Never* let your players do this. They can easily injure their necks or backs. Also, the goal of a throw-in is to get the ball to your own teammate. It is impossible to be accurate when doing the flip-type throw-in. Moves like that should be done only in gymnastics.

The Basics

1. Rules are very simple on throw-ins. Both feet must be on the ground when the ball is thrown, the hands must be directly over the head, and the ball must be thrown straight with equal pressure on each side (cannot spin right or left).

2. A perfectly thrown ball spins forward, directly to the player.
3. To throw, place one hand on each side of the ball, just back of center. Looking at your hands, the thumbs and index fingers will form a letter *W*.
4. Bring the ball back so it is over and behind your head.
5. Throw the ball onto the field, to your teammate, making sure the ball does not twist to the right or left.
6. The throw can be to a player's head, feet, or chest. The ball can also be directed back to the player that threw the ball. If you are going to do this, throw the ball and then step into the field of play to receive or kick the ball.

Note: Referees will call a bad throw and give the ball to the opposing team if the player throwing the ball throws it over one side or the other of her head. The ball must come directly over the top of the head.

Throw-In Drills

Line Throw (F)

Preparation: This requires the entire team and enough soccer balls for half of them.

Execution: Place the players in two parallel lines facing each other. Give the players on one side the balls. Have those players throw the balls to the players opposite them on the field. Then have those players return

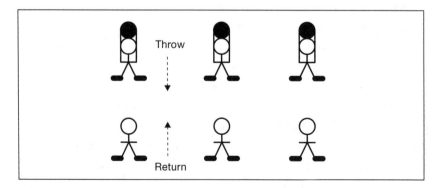

Figure 11.1 Line Throw

the balls in the same way. Walk up and down the field in between the players, observing their throws and making corrections as required. As the players develop, increase the distance between the lines. This teaches the basic throw-in.

Throw and Return (F)

Preparation: This requires two players and one ball.

Execution: Have the players face each other. Have one player throw the ball to the other player. Then have that player return the ball. Start with them trying to get the ball to each other with just three bounces, then two, then one. To make this intermediate level, have the players throw to the chest, head, or feet. The player receiving the ball will use the trapping/receiving techniques. To make it a game-level situation, place a defender between the two offensive players. This teaches the proper technique and the accuracy needed for throw-ins.

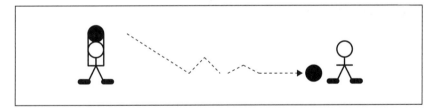

Figure 11.2 Throw and Return

To the Spot (I/G)

Preparation: This requires six players and one ball.

Execution: Place one person near the touchline with the ball. Place the other five players at different positions around the field. Have the player behind the touchline throw the ball to each, working on accuracy. After the player throws to each a few times, have another player do the throwing. Depending upon how many players you have, you can change the numbers so all of your players are involved at the same time. You can set up two or more groups and walk through and observe them while they are doing the drill. To make a game situation, use five players on the field to receive the ball and two to three defenders. This makes the players on the field move to get open and trains the player throwing to watch and make quick decisions on where to throw. Overall, this drill teaches accuracy, proper technique, and decision making.

Figure 11.3 To the Spot

12

Volley Instruction and Drills

A volley is a type of kick that happens when the ball is kicked while it is in the air. A half volley is the same type of kick, but after the ball has bounced. This is a power kick—very accurate and very hard to defend. When the volley is done correctly, the ball will travel forward with top-spin (top to bottom) and will curve down as it travels. When it hits the ground, it will shoot forward with the spin. If it hits an uneven area it can move right or left.

The Basics

1. Volleys are simple to do, and they are very effective.
2. To do a volley, one foot must be planted on the ground. The upper portion of your other leg is in the air, perpendicular with your body, and the lower portion of your leg is pointing toward the ground.
3. Your kicking foot must be pointing down with your ankle locked.
4. As the ball approaches, bring the lower half of your leg back and strike the ball sharply. Do not follow through on the kick; this will cause the ball to go into the air. Just quickly strike the ball and bring your leg back.

Volley Drills

Throw and Kick, Half Volley (F)

Preparation: This requires two players and one ball.

Execution: Have two players stand facing each other. Have one player throw the ball to the other player, on a bounce. As the ball bounces and starts coming down, have the second player move to be centered on the ball and tap it with his foot using the volley technique. At this time, technique is more important than power. Have the player do this 10 times, and then switch players so the person who was throwing is now kicking. This teaches the proper way to volley the ball.

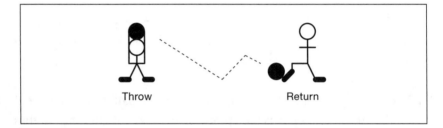

Throw   Return

Figure 12.1 **Throw and Kick, Half Volley**

Throw and Kick, Volley (F)

Preparation: This requires two players and one ball.

Execution: Have two players stand facing each other. Have one player throw the ball to the other player. As the ball starts coming down, have the second player move to be centered on the ball and tap it with her foot using the volley technique. Again, power is not important; technique

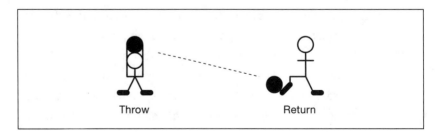

Throw   Return

Figure 12.2 **Throw and Kick, Volley**

is what matters. Have the player do this 10 times, and then switch players so the person who was throwing is now kicking. This teaches the proper way to center on the ball and then volley the ball accurately.

Volley on Goal (I)

Preparation: This drill uses all of the players, two balls, a goalkeeper, and a goal.

Execution: Put the players in two lines. You and an assistant throw the balls to the players at the front of the lines on a bounce. Put your goalkeeper in the goal to field the balls. Have the players shoot on goal. Start with the players close to the goal, and move them back as they improve. After each player has done a half volley a few times, move forward and toss the ball so they can do a full volley. Be careful; many times the ball will come back right at you. Be prepared. This teaches the players to volley while shooting at the goal and away from the goalkeeper.

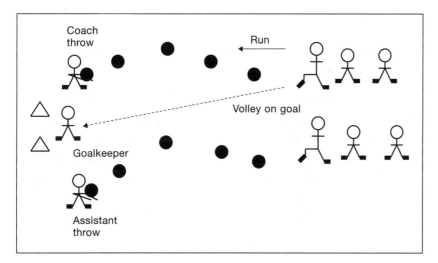

Figure 12.3 Volley on Goal

Volley with Defense (G)

Preparation: This requires a ball, a goalkeeper, one or two defenders, the rest of the team, and a goal.

Execution: Line up the players behind the penalty box line. The first person in line will be the first to kick. Have the second player in line throw the ball over the first player's head toward the goal. Have the player move on the ball and volley it toward the goal. Put a defender or two in the goal box. As the ball is thrown, the defenders may also move to the ball. Let each player run a couple of repetitions of this. This teaches the players to volley while under defensive pressure.

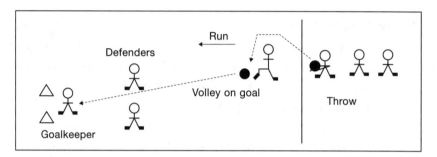

***Figure 12.4* Volley with Defense**

Kick and Volley (F)

Preparation: This requires all the players, a ball, and a goal. This can be done with or without a goalkeeper.

Execution: Line up the players in single file in front of the goal. The first player in line will be the first to kick and should face the second person in line, who has the ball. Have the second person throw the ball to the feet of the person getting ready to kick. The kicker kicks the ball up and over his head and then turns, moves to the ball, and volleys on goal. This sounds difficult, but it is not. It is fun and easy to do, and it builds confidence. This develops ball control and teaches the players to locate and play the ball.

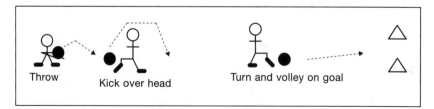

***Figure 12.5* Kick and Volley**

13

Goalkeeping Instruction and Drills

The goalkeeper is a key element to the defense. This person is required to have the skills of the players on the field and the additional skills required for defending the goal. Make sure your goalie practices the field skills with the other players during practice. With younger teams, do not stick one player in the goal and leave her there. Younger players need to develop all skills. Leaving one person in the goal hampers her field techniques. Develop multiple goalkeepers for the younger teams. As the players advance in age and skill, goalkeeper skills will become evident.

The goalkeeper is the captain of the defense and must be able to direct the fullbacks and other players to make a strong and responsive team.

The Basics

1. Do not be afraid of the ball. Learn to anticipate where it is going, and then you can control it.
2. Work all of the penalty area. Do not just stay in front of the goal. If you can get to the ball anywhere in the penalty area, go for it.
3. Dive and jump only when necessary. If you catch the ball you are OK, but

if you don't, you are on the ground and are unable to respond to the movement of the ball.

4. Cut the angle. This means move with the ball to decrease the amount of open goal.

Note: As shown in Figure 13.1, if the ball is moved to the side (1), the goalkeeper (GK) has a very small area to cover. As the ball moves to the center of the field (2), it creates a wider area to defend. If the GK (a) stays in the mouth of the goal, there is a wide area to the goalie's right and left. As the goalie moves away from the goal (b), toward the ball, the area of open goal is decreased.

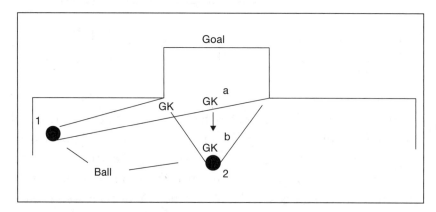

Figure 13.1 Cut the Angle

Goalkeeping Drills

Figure Eight (F)

Preparation: This requires a goalkeeper and a soccer ball.

Execution: This exercise is to learn to handle the ball and obtain greater ball control. Have the goalkeeper stand up, spread his legs, and place the soccer ball on the outside of his right knee using his right hand. He should move the ball in front of the knee and behind the left knee where the ball is taken by the left hand. Keep the ball moving by going around to the front of the left knee and then behind the right knee.

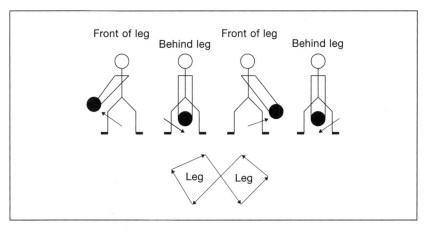

Figure 13.2 **Figure Eight**

This movement around the knees is in the form of a figure eight. Keep this movement continuous. This develops ball handling and quickness.

Drop and Catch (F)

Preparation: This requires a goalkeeper and a soccer ball.

Execution: Have the goalkeeper stand up, spread her legs, and place the ball between both knees with one hand on the front of the ball and the other hand on the back of the ball. She should drop the ball and quickly reverse the position of the hands (moving the front hand to the back of the ball and the back hand to the front of the ball) to catch the ball before the ball hits the ground. Do at least 25 repetitions of this drill each practice. This develops touch and quickness.

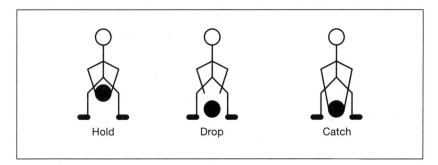

Figure 13.3 **Drop and Catch**

Throw and Catch (F)

Preparation: This requires a goalkeeper and a soccer ball.

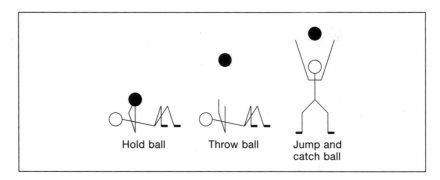

Hold ball   Throw ball   Jump and
                                        catch ball

Figure 13.4 Throw and Catch

Execution: Have the goalkeeper lie on his back and throw the ball as high as he can into the air. The goalkeeper then jumps up and catches the ball before it touches the ground. Do 10 repetitions of this drill each practice. This teaches movement, strength, eye contact, and touch on the ball.

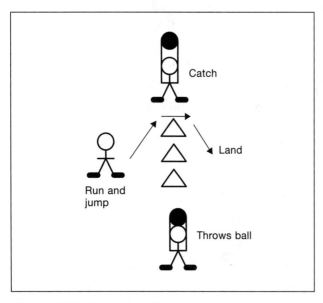

Catch

Run and
jump

Land

Throws ball

Figure 13.5 Jump over Cones

Jump over Cones (I)

Preparation: This requires a goal-keeper, three cones, another player to throw the ball, and a soccer ball.

Execution: Place three cones side by side on the field. Have the goalkeeper run toward the front (widest side) of the cones. As the goalkeeper reaches the cones, have the other player throw the ball into the air. The goalie must jump to clear the cones and at the same time catch the ball. This develops timing and ball control.

Jump and Catch (G)

Preparation: This requires a goalkeeper, cones, two additional players for each set of cones, and a soccer ball.

Execution: Place three sets of cones (two wide) with about five steps between each set of cones. Have players stand on each side of the cones (all three sets) with enough clearance for the goalkeeper to jump over the cones. Have the goalkeeper run toward the first set of cones. As the goalie approaches, have the player on one side throw the ball. Have the player on the other side try to head the ball, while at the same time the goalkeeper tries to catch the ball. Continue through all three sets of cones without stopping. Repeat this as many times as is required for the goalie to concentrate on the ball and not the other players. This develops concentration and ball control.

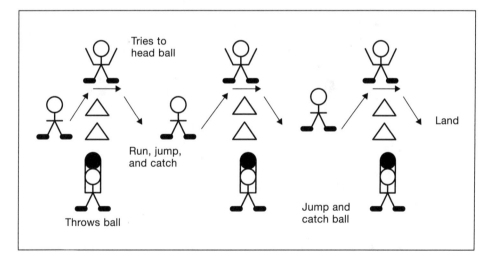

Figure 13.6 Jump and Catch

Skill Development

To develop overall movement and techniques needed for the goalkeeper, individual skills must be developed.

Lie and Punch (F)

When the ball is kicked toward the goal and is high, the goalkeeper needs to punch the ball straight up. The speed and momentum of the ball will carry it forward. Punching the ball will cause it to rise and go over the top of the goal. Make sure the goalkeeper does not try to grab high balls, just clear them.

Preparation: This requires the goalkeeper, another player, and a soccer ball.

Execution: Have the goalkeeper lie on her back. Have the other player throw the ball underhanded to the goalie. The goalie, with hands made into a fist, will punch the ball straight up. This teaches the goalkeeper how to clear balls that are out of reach.

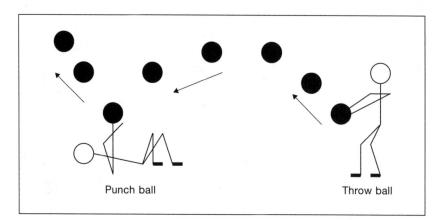

Punch ball   Throw ball

Figure 13.7 **Lie and Punch**

Stand and Punch (F)

Preparation: This requires the goalkeeper, another player, and a soccer ball.

Execution: This is identical to the Lie and Punch, except the goalkeeper is standing up and the ball is thrown, underhanded, so it is above the goalkeeper, making the goalie jump up and punch the ball.

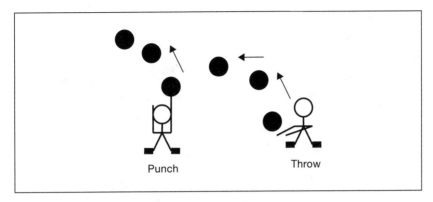

Punch

Throw

Figure 13.8 **Stand and Punch**

Dive (Sitting, Kneeling, Standing) (F/I/G)

Preparation: This requires the goalkeeper, two other players, and a soccer ball.

Execution: Have the goalkeeper sit on the ground, with his legs straight in front of himself. Roll the ball to the right and then the left side of the goalkeeper, and have him lean over with the top of his body and with his arms reach out and stop the ball. The goalkeeper's hands are placed so one hand is behind the ball and one is on top of the ball. If the ball is close, it can be wrapped into the arms, but in either case it must be stopped and held to the ground before it is gathered into the arms. To move this to the intermediate level, have the goalie get on his knees. Repeat rolling the ball (slowly) to the left and right of the goalkeeper, and have the goalkeeper roll to his right or left to stop the ball. It is important at this time to make sure the goalkeeper is falling on the ball to break his dive. He should not dive straight out and fall without support. To make this a game situation, have the goalkeeper stand, and have another player kick the ball (slowly) to the right and left while the goalie dives to catch the ball. Pick up speed as the goalie improves, and then add a defender so the goalkeeper gets used to having players moving through his field of vision. This teaches the techniques used in diving for the ball.

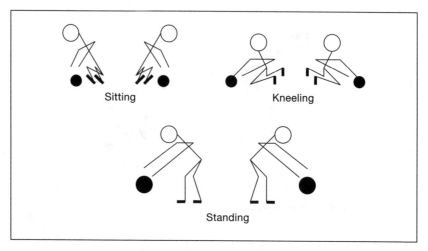

Sitting   Kneeling

Standing

Figure 13.9 Dive

Trap and Scoop (G)

Preparation: This requires the goalkeeper, another player, a soccer ball, and a goal.

Execution: Have the goalkeeper stand in front of the goal. Have another player kick the ball on the ground, directly at the goalie. To properly field a ground ball the goalkeeper will go down to her knees so her legs are in place to block the ball if she misses it with her hands. When the ball is on the ground to the left or right, the goalkeeper will go down on one knee with the other leg out in front of her to block the ball. When the ball comes directly at the goalie, the goalie will extend her arms out and make an area for the ball to run up her arms (arms extended, arms together, palms facing up, fingers pointing out). As the ball rolls into her hands, she should scoop up the ball by grabbing it with her hands and folding her arms into her chest. This protects the ball and enables the goalkeeper to have complete control.

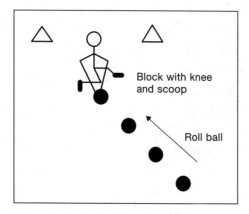

Block with knee and scoop

Roll ball

Figure 13.10 Trap and Scoop

14

Offensive and Defensive Drills

Drills that incorporate and enhance the skills and techniques that the players have learned are a necessity to move your team forward and make them competitive. Don't just scrimmage all of the time; these drills can hone the on-field skills and techniques, getting all of the players involved. The more the players touch the ball, the better they will be.

Offensive and Defensive Drills

Centering (G)

The perfect goal attempt is when the players bring the ball down the right or left side of the field and then center the ball to the players in the center of the field. This spreads the defense and also has them moving backward toward their own goal. Practice makes this move practical.

Preparation: This requires one soccer ball, three offensive players, one goalkeeper, two defenders, and a goal.

Execution: Line up the three offensive players so one player is on the outside near the touchline and the other two are even with the outside lines of the penalty box. Have one defensive player on the outside to play man-to-man against whoever gets the ball— the outside offensive player or the one in the center of the field. Make sure the goalkeeper moves in relation to the ball. Have the outside offensive player bring the ball down the field toward the end line. When the player gets near the end line, he should center the ball (kick the ball to the center of the field). Have the two other offensive players get into a position to shoot on goal. The defensive player needs to try to take the ball away or clear the ball out of the goal area. Make sure the player centering the ball from the right-hand side uses the right foot to center. If centering from the left, the player should use the left foot to center.

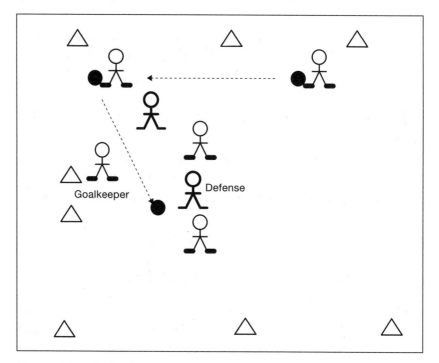

Figure 14.1 Centering

Throw and Shoot (G)

Players need to be able to quickly move on the ball and shoot without hesitation. Most players will want to get the ball just perfect for a shot. By the time they get it perfect, they have lost the advantage. This drill prepares the players to shoot instantly.

Preparation: This requires one ball, 10 cones, four offensive players, and a goalkeeper. You can also add two defenders.

Execution: Set up the cones so there are two in the center to represent the goal and four on each side of the goalkeeper for the offensive players to stand in. Set up the four offensive players in pairs of two. Place these two sets of cones and players approximately 30 yards from each other. The goalkeeper is in the center between these sets of players. One of the offensive players gets inside the cones, and the other offensive player (outside the cones) throws the ball inside the cones and in front of the second player. That player moves quickly to the ball and shoots before the ball can roll very far. It may be necessary for the player to settle (gain control of) the ball before shooting. Do not allow more than two touches on the ball to control it. The player shoots at the two cones used for the goal, and the goalkeeper tries to stop or catch the ball. The goalkeeper then throws the ball to the other outside offensive player, and the action is repeated from the other side. Change the shooters and throwers every time the ball returns. Adding a defender at each side puts pressure on the offensive players and causes them to shoot faster.

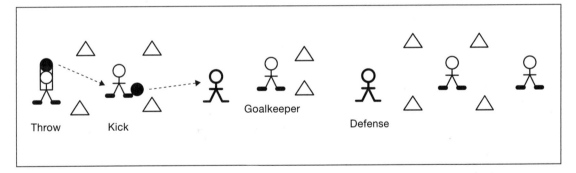

Figure 14.2 Throw and Shoot

Throw into Box and Kick (G)
This drill is similar to Throw and Shoot. It uses the same setup and teaches the same quick-shoot skills. The more the players practice these drills, the more accurate they will become.

Preparation: This requires one ball, 10 cones, four offensive players, and a goalkeeper. You can also add two defenders.

Execution: Set up the cones so that there are two in the center to represent the goal and four on each side of the goalkeeper for the offensive players to use. Set up the four offensive players in pairs of two. Place these two sets of players approximately 30 yards from each other. Place the goalkeeper in the center between these sets of players. Have both of the offensive players stand outside and at the far end of the cones. One offensive player throws the ball inside the cones, and the other player runs inside the cones. That player moves quickly to the ball and shoots before the ball can roll very far. It may be necessary for the player to settle the ball before shooting. Do not allow more than two touches on the ball to control it. The player shoots at the two cones used for the goal, and the goalkeeper tries to stop or catch the ball. The goalkeeper then throws the ball to the other outside offensive players, and the action is repeated from the other side. Change the shooters and throwers every time the ball returns. Adding a defender at each side puts pressure on the offensive players and causes them to shoot faster. This drill can be changed by having the players shoot with only one touch or having them shoot on the bounce.

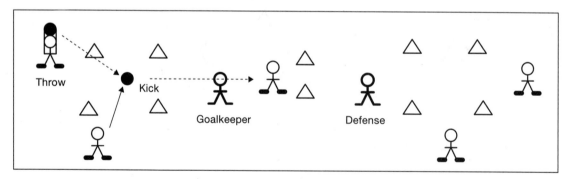

Figure 14.3 Throw into Box and Kick

Over the Goal (G)

Here is a drill that I have seen used by many different teams. It is another shooting drill that teaches the players to move to the ball quickly and shoot. It does require the use of a goal.

Preparation: This drill uses one goal, one ball, team players, and a goalkeeper.

Execution: Line up the players facing the goal and approximately 15 yards (minimum) away from the goal. Put the goalkeeper in the goal. As the coach, you will take the ball and stand behind the goal. Throw the ball over the goal, and have the players quickly move on the ball and shoot. Have the goalkeeper also move on the ball. Players who miss the goal with the ball must go get it and then get back into line.

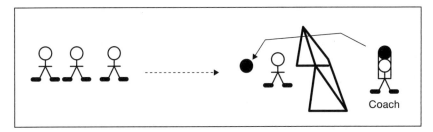

Figure 14.4 **Over the Goal**

One-on-One (G)

The ability to play both offense and defense is a necessity. As with the other drills in the book, this one is designed to allow the players to have fun. When you first start this drill, group the players by skill. Place them as stronger with stronger and weaker with weaker. As the players get comfortable with this drill, mix their skill levels. This drill places the offensive and defensive players one-on-one and moving down the field to the goal.

Preparation: This requires three players, two cones, and one ball.

Execution: Place the cones so they are set up in a goal configuration. Put two of the players about 30 yards out from the goal, having them stand side by side, and give them the ball. Designate one as offense and one as defense. Place the other player in the goal as the goalkeeper. After every attempt on goal, have the players rotate so they all play all three positions. Blow the whistle to start play. The player with the ball will move toward the goal while the defensive player tries to take the ball away. If the defensive player takes the ball away, that player now becomes offense, and the player that lost the ball becomes defense. Keep this up until one of the players shoots on goal. This can also be done on a full scale by putting your players on the centerline and moving toward the goal. Use your goalkeeper if it is full-scale; otherwise, the goalkeeper does the drill just like everyone else.

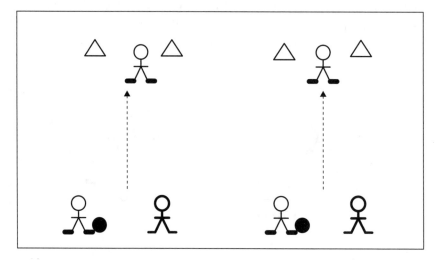

Figure 14.5 One-on-One

Back and Forth (G)
This drill uses offensive and defensive skills. It also encourages team-work and promotes accuracy rather than power. It requires the players to move to open space, pass, receive, and play offense and defense. In other words, it does it all.

Preparation: This requires one ball, six players, and six cones.

Execution: Divide the players into two teams. Place two offensive play-ers at one end, one offensive player and one defensive player in the cen-ter, and two defenders (one who will be the goalkeeper) at the other end of the drill area. Place the players with approximately 15 yards between each set of two players. Have one of the offensive players at the end pass to their teammate in the center. That player has to move to get open to receive the pass. The defensive player in the center tries to intercept or stop the pass. When the player gets the ball, the player moves toward the other end and tries to score. The defense tries to take the ball away,

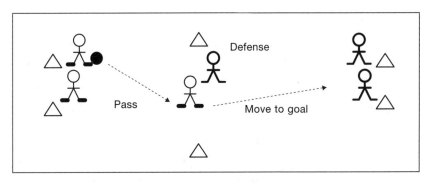

Figure 14.6 **Back and Forth**

and the person playing goalkeeper tries to stop the shot. Rotate players after there has been an attempt at both ends of the practice area.

The Ultimate Challenge (G)

This is a difficult drill to complete, but it can and will be accomplished successfully by your players. This drill builds skill and confidence and also teaches offensive and defensive skills against other players.

Preparation: This requires one ball, four players, and eight cones.

Execution: Lay out the cones so they make three squares, back to back, 10 yards long by 10 yards across. As the skill of the players increases, the area can be reduced. Place one player inside each of the squares. This 10-yard square area is the area the player inside the square defends. The players cannot leave their squares. The fourth player then tries to dribble through all three squares without losing the ball. As the offensive player goes into another square, the next defender picks up the play.

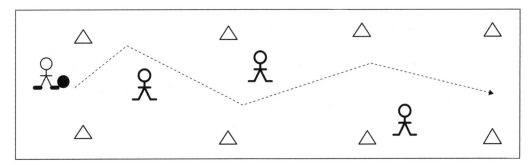

Figure 14.7 **The Ultimate Challenge**

Cutthroat (G)

This drill places three players on the field, each trying to get the ball and get to his own area. The players must work as teams and separately, developing their skills in offense and defense.

Preparation: This requires one ball, three players, and three cones.

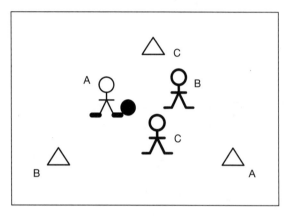

Figure 14.8 Cutthroat

Execution: Place the three cones so they form a triangle, with about 15 yards between each cone. If you have space constraints, less space between the cones is OK. Put all three players in the center of the cone area. Throw out the ball. Each player has a designated cone and must get to his cone or shoot and hit his cone to score. The other two players try to get the ball and do the same. You will find that the two players without the ball will play as a team until one gets the ball, and then the other two will play as a team.

Three vs. Three (G)

This drill incorporates all aspects of the game. It uses three players on each team, but no goalkeeper. Playing without a goalkeeper forces the players to play a strong defense to keep the other team from scoring. You can set up multiple teams playing at the same time. Depending on how many players you have on the team, you can increase to four vs. four or five vs. five to ensure all of your players can play at the same time.

Preparation: This drill uses one ball, eight cones, and six players.

Execution: Set up the field just like a regular soccer field, except place the cones so they make a goal that is three feet across, and make the length of the field much shorter—under 30 yards long. Have one set of three players kick off while the other set of three players defends their goal. Put a 10-minute limit on the game. This is fast-paced, and you may have to stop if the players get too tired.

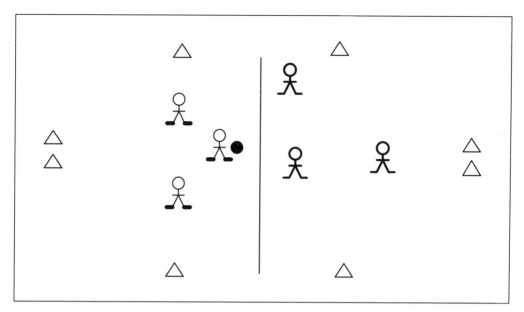

***Figure 14.9* Three vs. Three**

Keeping the Players in Formation (G)

One of the most difficult challenges you will have to face is keeping the players from chasing after the ball. They will want to move and group around the ball rather than keep their positions.

Preparation: This uses one ball, numerous cones, brightly colored outdoor electrical cord (25 to 50 feet), and two teams of players.

Execution: Set up the field just like a regular soccer field, except place the cones so they also go down the center (length) of the field. Lay the electrical cord directly down the center (width) of the field to divide the field into two. (You can use anything to divide the field. I had 50-foot and 25-foot orange electrical cords. So I connected them and used them.) Put your players in the playing formation you will be using. Make sure the players on the right half of the field stay in their half and the players on the left half of the field stay in their own half. They cannot go across the centerline; they must stop at the line and wait for the ball to cross back over to their side. The center players can go onto either side but should not go to the outer touchlines. At this point, have one

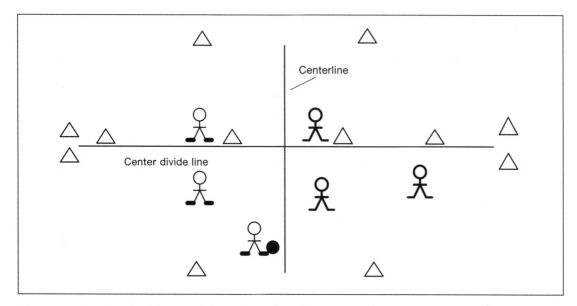

Figure 14.10 Keeping the Players in Formation

team bring the ball down the field just as in a game. Observe your players to ensure they are keeping their positions. Stop play by blowing the whistle when individual players go out of position. This teaches the players to better hold their positions, giving a start to good formation play.

Penalty Kick Swap (G)

This drill is great to use when you want your players to be working but also resting. It can be done at any time in practice—beginning, middle, or end.

Preparation: This requires one ball, cones or goal, and all of the players.

Execution: Put one person in the goal. Line up all of the other players so they are behind the penalty mark. Each player kicks a penalty kick. If the person kicking scores, that person goes back into line to kick again. If the player misses the goal or the ball is stopped by the person in the goal, then the person that kicked becomes the goalkeeper. The person that was the goalkeeper goes into the line to kick. This is fast-paced, and the players like to do the drill. It also lets you know who your best penalty kickers are. This teaches kicking accuracy and enables your players to rest in between the kicks.

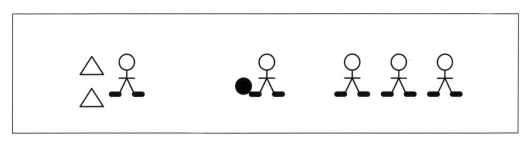

Figure 14.11 **Penalty Kick Swap**

15

Basic Skills and Individual Technique Drills

Individual Practice

Give your players these drills to do as homework. Ask them to use the plastic bag for five minutes and to juggle until they reach a certain number of kicks—5, 10, or 20, depending on age and skill.

Plastic Bag

This teaches the proper placement of the kick and builds strength.

The best way to practice kicking is by placing the soccer ball in a large plastic bag and having the player hold onto the top of the bag so the ball cannot come out of the bag. While standing, walking, or running, the player should continuously kick the ball. The player can tell if it is a good kick by the way the ball travels away from the kick. If it goes to the side or twists, it is a bad kick. If it goes straight out and back, it is a good kick. This is a good way to practice alone; a player can get a kick every second. Kicking the ball against a building, wall, or fence or to another person limits the kicks. More can be accomplished in minutes with the bag than in hours with other people.

Juggling

This teaches ball control and touch.

The player should drop the ball onto her foot (or thigh or head), and then pop the ball back into the air. She must keep the ball moving up and down without using her hands. When the player is juggling the ball with her feet, thighs (just above the knees), or head, she should keep the ball at a constant low level while watching the ball very closely. She should not hit it really hard and high into the air. The player should see how many times she can touch the ball without the ball touching the ground.

16

Game Strategy and Drills

Defense

Defense is the foundation of soccer. A perfectly played defensive soccer game is one with a score of 0–0. However, games are won by demonstrating outstanding defense and having a great offense that is able to overcome the other team's defense. Remember, if your team cannot get the ball, they cannot score. Some teams will train their players to play only offense or defense. Proper training and play has all players playing defense when the other team has the ball and offense when their team has the ball.

Immediate Chase

Players who lose the ball must immediately go after the ball.

The person who loses the ball is the first to go after the ball. That player is the closest, and it is very important that he apply pressure on the person who now has the ball. This means he tries to get the ball back as quickly as he can and allows the other members of the team to recover and get into their defensive positions without giving free run on the field to the person who now has the ball. Delaying the person is a must. Putting pressure on the person who has the ball can cause a takeaway or force a bad pass.

Fall Back and Delay

While the player is giving immediate chase, the rest of the team falls back, challenges the person with the ball, and delays that person from getting into their team's goal area.

The most dangerous place on the field is the center, so have your players force the person with the ball toward the touchline. This limits the person's ability to pass and limits the directions the person can go.

Arc of Concentration

The arc of concentration is the area that is the most dangerous for scoring. The majority of the goals scored are scored while in the arc area. It is important to concentrate on moving the ball outside of this area.

As you can see in Figure 16.1, the arc is in front of the goal and goes from the corner post of the goal through the corner of the goal box and continues out to the touchline. Any time the ball is in this area, the

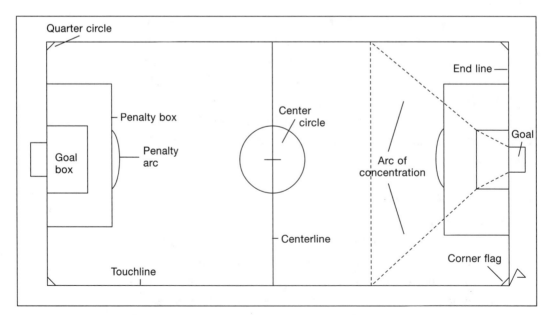

Figure 16.1 Arc of Concentration

chances for scoring increase. Emphasize to your team that they must clear the ball from this area as quickly as possible. They should not ever play with the ball in this area. Most defenders will receive the ball and move to their left or right (closest direction) toward the touchline before passing or clearing the ball.

Balance

Balance is important to the defense. This is how the team addresses the other team's players—in other words, how they play in relation to the person with the ball.

The players that are nearest to the ball will play tight, meaning they stay as close to the ball as they can. The players that are away from the ball play loose, which means they put themselves in a position to cover any possibilities and not just one person. They cover a specific area.

Control

It is important to get the ball back as quickly as possible. Your team is in control when they have the ball. If the other team has the ball, you will lack the control.

Get the ball away from the opposing player as quickly and efficiently as you can. Many players try to tackle the ball (slide into the ball, without touching the other player, to knock the ball away from the opponent). This is often a mistake. If the players miss the ball, they are now on the ground, and the other player is on the way toward the goal with the ball. Tackle only when necessary.

Midfield Play

Most games are won in the midfield battles. If you cannot win the ball at the midfield, then you cannot advance the ball forward. Always losing the ball at midfield means your team is on defense all of the time. Eventually the other team will score in this situation.

Get Possession

It is a must to gain possession of the ball. Once your player gets the ball, have her dribble to open space, away from the other team's players. Dribbling to open space allows the rest of your team to get open. As soon as your player gets out of traffic, she must use passes to move the ball quickly. It is best to have the other team chasing the ball. They can keep up with a person dribbling the ball, but they cannot run as fast as the ball can be passed. Use the whole team when you are passing. Pass backward to the fullbacks, forward to your forwards, or sideways to other midfielders. Anyone open is the right person to pass the ball to. Keep changing the direction of the ball. Don't always pass forward or backward. Move it around, and keep the other team moving. When the other players are moving and do not know where the ball is going, they cannot set up an adequate defense, and you have the advantage.

Attack

To take the ball away from the other team, your players must be aggressive. They must go after the person with the ball so your team can get possession. This means they must stop the player with the ball from moving to open space. If one player can stop the player with the ball, then another player from your team can assist and double-team the player to get the ball. When your players get the ball, they should stay on the attack, but now as offense. They should move quickly to open space to avoid being trapped.

Offense

As in defense, when the team goes on offense, all players are on offense. With your defense solid, it is important to break down the other team's defense so your team can score. This is done by using techniques different from those used on defense.

Mobility

It is important that the offense be mobile. Your players must keep moving and keep the other team's defense off balance.

As stated previously, when your players get the ball, they must move to open space. This is the only way they will be able to get open to get the ball to their teammates. Moving the ball constantly throws off the defense, and this is what you want. You want to be in control by having the other team responding to what your players are doing on the field. Constantly moving the ball creates open spots. Your players and the ball must be in continuous motion.

Runs

Players cannot be predictable. Emphasize that they must be creative. The players on the other team can never know what your players are going to do. The opposing players will pick up on what is happening after a player does the same thing once or twice. If they figure out that players do the same thing every time, the other team will set up to stop the person. As a result, your players must vary what they do on the field.

There are many different ways to effectively move the ball. Your players are limited only by their own imagination. The diagonal run, where the player moves diagonally across the field rather than straight, advances the ball but causes the defense to adjust. The blind-side run is when the player with the ball goes to the back side of the player that is providing defense. The on-side run is going directly in front of the defensive player.

Bending or curving is going right and left, moving like the curves in a road; this does not allow the defense to keep up with the player who has the ball. Because the player who has the ball knows what she wants to do, she can do it at any time. The defense is constantly kept off balance by the person curving or bending around the field.

Perhaps the most effective is the start-and-stop run. When dribbling, it is important to change your speed. Stopping and then quickly starting again and going in a different direction causes the defense to stay in pursuit. The other team is unable to effectively establish a strong defense.

Support

At all times, the members of your team must be in a position to support their teammates. I prefer to teach the diamond (triangle) method. It is easy to understand and easy to execute. Figure 16.2 shows a full team of 11. The *P* is a player, and the *G* is the goalkeeper. This method can be done for players of any age, no matter how many there are. Although not every position in the diagram has dotted lines connecting them, it is easy to see that everyone makes up a triangle or a full diamond. As

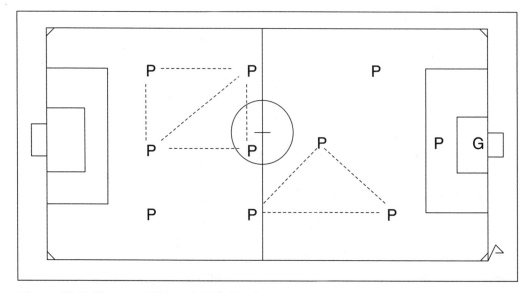

Figure 16.2 **Diamond (Triangle) Method**

long as the players stay in this general formation, the person with the ball will always have a place to pass the ball. This can be in any direction.

When a player gets the ball, he must have at least two players to whom he can pass. When the players are on the same side of the field as the ball (strong side), they must move into a triangle formation to get open for the player with the ball. The players on the other side of the field (weak side) must be moving to be able to make runs so the ball can be switched from one side of the field (strong) to the other side of the field (weak). The advantage to this is there will be less of a defense on the weak side of the field. Switching the ball is very effective.

The best way to practice defense, midfield play, offense, and support is to run drills incorporating the principles listed in this chapter (see Figure 16.3). Do not just scrimmage, but run a drill with emphasis on the area you want to train. Stop the drill to make corrections and compliments, and then repeat until it becomes automatic for the players.

Starting with defense, put your players in a 4-3-3 formation (see Chapter 17), and then select players to play offense. You will need five or six to run the offense and six plus the goalkeeper to run the defense.

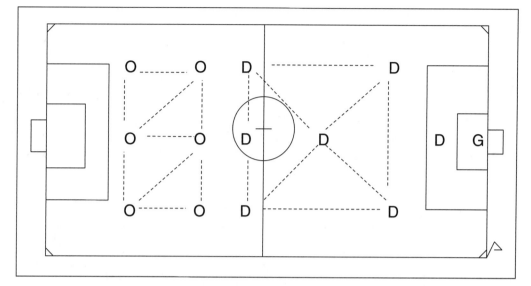

Figure 16.3 **Starting Drill Formation**

As you can see in Figure 16.4, the offensive and midfield players shift to adjust for the ball coming down the left side. The defense also shifted to compensate for the movement of the ball. Both sides maintained their triangle formations to give support. You can stop at any time to make

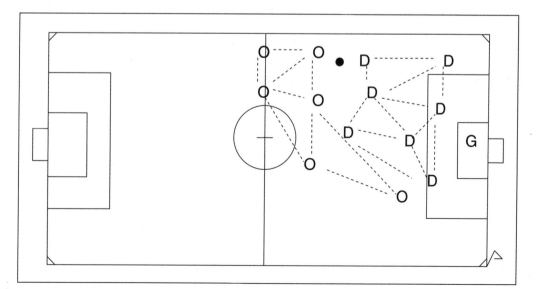

Figure 16.4 **Ball Moving Down the Left Side**

corrections and adjustments and then restart the drill. While the drill is running, encourage the offensive players to make diagonal runs, blind-side runs, on-side runs, and bending and curving runs and to change their speed.

Figure 16.5 shows the ball centered. Upon the completion of the center, stop the play and repeat.

The remaining player positions have been added into the diagram and are underlined. This is what it would look like if all 22 players were on the field.

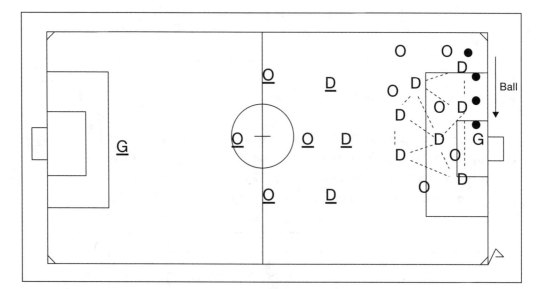

Figure 16.5 **Ball Centered from the Left Side**

17

Formations
and Drills

A formation is how the players are positioned on the field, and formations are the backbone of soccer. You must perform drills using the formations so your players will know how to react on the field. This chapter covers standard formations. Place your players in the appropriate formation and run the formation as you would any other drill. You are not playing a real soccer game; you are drilling your players on proper position and reaction to the location and play of the ball. Run the formation drill, stop, make corrections, and run the drill again. Keep repeating until all of your players know how to react properly and maintain their position.

Formations

The formations are designed to provide the ultimate offense and defense. They are balanced throughout. Any arrangement that provides balance is acceptable. There are common formations, but sometimes you have to be creative and go with a special setup. If it works, then it is a good formation. Formations are designed to provide strong offense and defense with equal-strength players. If you do not have equal-strength players, then be creative. If you have strong forwards and half-backs but weaker fullbacks, then add fullbacks and decrease the number of forwards and/or halfbacks. The stronger players will compensate for the decreased numbers.

Formations are labeled by starting with the fullbacks and moving through the halfbacks to the forwards. The goalkeeper is not counted in the formation label. It is a balanced formation. If you are playing with fewer players (younger teams), just decrease the numbers in each area while still maintaining balance throughout the field.

The Under-6 rules vary by league. Some have six players on the field with no goalkeeper (six total), and some have six players on the field plus the goalkeeper (seven total). Under-8 normally plays with six players plus the goalkeeper (seven total). Under-10 usually plays with seven players plus a goalkeeper (eight total). The Under-12 and above teams use 11 players. Look at your league rules to ensure you are using the correct number of players.

Figure 17.1 is a formation of 11 players that gives strong offense and defense. The field is balanced.

The 4-3-3 formation allows four players in the fullback positions, three in the halfback positions, and three in the forward positions. The

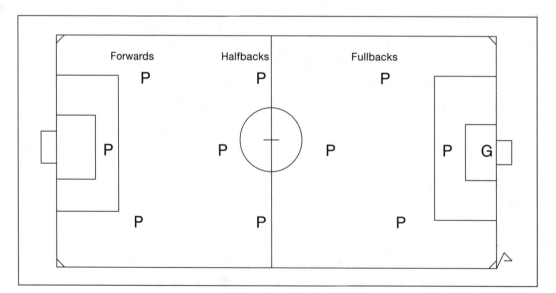

Figure 17.1 4-3-3 Formation, 11 Players

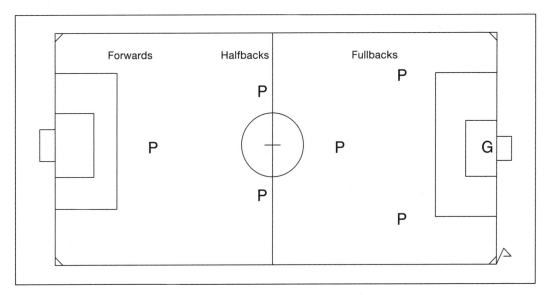

Figure 17.2 **3-2-1 Formation, 6 or 7 Players**

halfbacks can move easily from offense to defense. Quite often, scoring is done by a halfback moving into a scoring position and overloading the other team's defense. Many inexperienced and undertrained teams will concentrate just on stopping the forwards and forget that all players must play offense and defense. These teams are open to strikes made from the midfield. The halfbacks can also easily fall back to provide extra defense while the forwards delay and try to regain possession of the ball.

The 3-2-1 (Figure 17.2) is a good formation for U-6 and U-8 teams. It is easy for the players to keep their positions and provide good balance throughout the field. The U-6 and U-8 players have a tendency to play the ball rather than play a position. Run drills using this formation, stopping the play when necessary to point out where the players should be positioned. Don't get discouraged if you see a player across the field, away from the ball, drawing in the dirt. Remember, their attention span is short.

The 3-2-2 (Figure 17.3) is a very good balanced formation. Adding one player changes it to a 3-3-2 formation. You can also change it to a 4-2-2 formation if you have strong forwards and halfbacks but weaker fullbacks. It is also a formation you can go to if you get a strong lead and

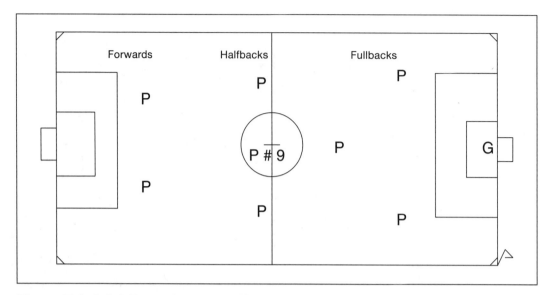

Figure 17.3 **3-2-2 Formation, 8 or 9 Players**

don't want to run up the score but want to keep the other team from scoring.

The 4-4-2 formation is one I often use in the second half. I start with the 4-3-3. That enables the team to provide strong balance in all areas.

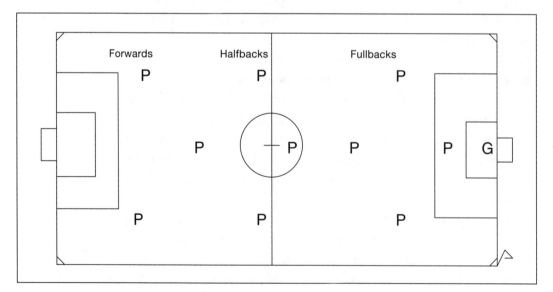

Figure 17.4 **4-4-2 Formation—Stronger Offense**

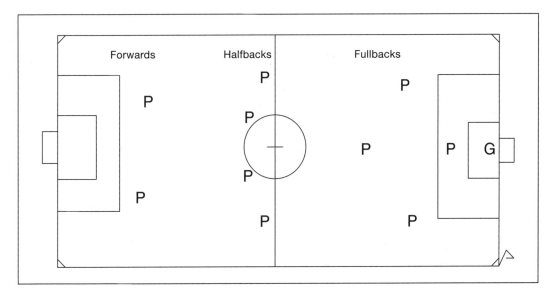

Figure 17.5 **4-2-2 Formation—Stronger Defense**

By halftime you normally know what weak points the opposing team has. Using the 4-4-2 allows the team to keep the opposing team out of your half of the field and yet provide strong offense by having the players make strikes out of the midfield. The layout of the 4-4-2 can be varied. The formation in Figure 17.4 resembles the 4-3-3; it shows strong balance throughout the field and gives a stronger offense. The formation in Figure 17.5 builds a curtain across the field using the halfbacks and gives a stronger defense. The difference is in the positioning of the players.

As stated earlier, all players must play both offense and defense. The formations that are listed in this chapter are common ones that provide good balance. However, you must be creative. I have played teams that had very strong center offense but limited defense. When I had just started in soccer, my team played another team that had us on the ropes. We were three points down at halftime, and my team was getting beat up. During halftime, I talked to the referee, who was a friend of mine and an adult soccer player. His advice was to be creative. He said I should use my team's strong points and capitalize on the other team's weak points. He went on to say that the formation I was using was inappropriate against this team. He suggested I go to a 6-2-2 formation (Fig-

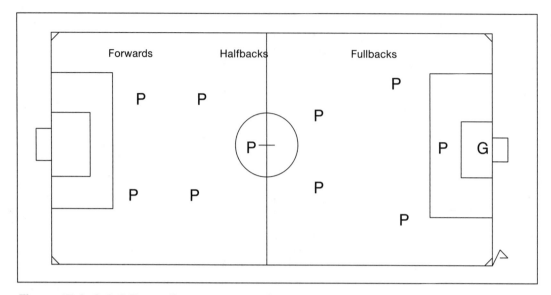
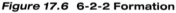

Figure 17.6 **6-2-2 Formation**

ure 17.6). I told him that I had never seen anything on a 6-2-2 formation. He just smiled and said, "You can use anything that works, and obviously the formation you are using is not working." The 6-2-2 formation worked that game and served its purpose. We made back the three points and the second half was a real soccer game, not a runaway.

Centering the Ball

One of the most effective ways to get the ball into the arc of concentration and to score is by centering the ball (kicking the ball from the side into the center of the field). This requires the rest of the team to be in perfect balance with the person centering the ball. Centering the ball is easy to do and is done on both sides of the field. This needs to be practiced by running centering drills—not a scrimmage, but a drill where the basics are taught. Ensure all of the principles of offense, midfield, defense, and support are emphasized.

When the player gets the ball, she moves it to the outside of the field and moves down the field toward the end line (see Figure 17.7). This can be done by passing or dribbling. It is important to get as close as pos-

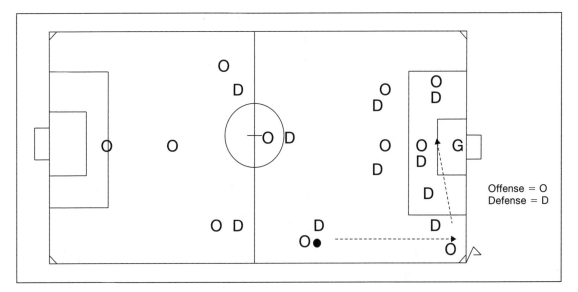

Figure 17.7 **Centering the Ball**

sible to the end line. When the ball is centered from or very near the end line, there is less chance of being offside because the person actually receiving the ball is even with or behind where the kick originated. By taking the ball to the outside near the touchline and centering the ball, your team also spreads out the defense, affecting their balance. To properly protect the goal, the defense has to collapse to put a line in between the person centering the ball and the goal. When the players are spread out, the defense is at its weakest point. When your team is on defense, tell them to keep their formation as much as possible and to clear the ball quickly.

Kickoff and Receiving Formations

Kicking off and receiving are not done often, so don't spend all of your time working these formations. However, with that said, your team needs to run drills so they know what to do when they have to do it. It is important to teach the basics of these formations to your team. Run drills using the formations listed. It is not necessary to run the ball all the way to the goal. Just run the drill as far as necessary to ensure everyone on offense and defense knows what they are doing.

When you are teaching your team formations, just use one that is simple for the players to grasp. You need only three formations to start:

- Playing formation
- Kickoff formation
- Receiving formation

The kickoff and receiving formations can be taught easily. These formations are just variations of the playing formation. Remember that the ball has to roll forward at least one rotation before it can be touched by another player. The original player cannot touch the ball again until it has been touched by a second player.

Kickoff Formations

Many younger teams just go to the center circle and kick the ball as hard as they can. This is their kickoff strategy. It can work, but normally it just gives the ball to the opposing team. The advantages of just kicking the ball as hard as you can are simple:

- It gets the ball close to the opponent's goal.
- If kicked to the right or left side, it enables your team to work a smaller area.
- It is simple to teach your team to kick and then take off.

These are the disadvantages:

- You lose control of the ball.
- Your team normally converges on the ball and loses their formation (balance).
- It doesn't teach the team ball control or working together.

My preference is to roll the ball forward to your teammate and then move the ball to the outside of the field and then down the field toward

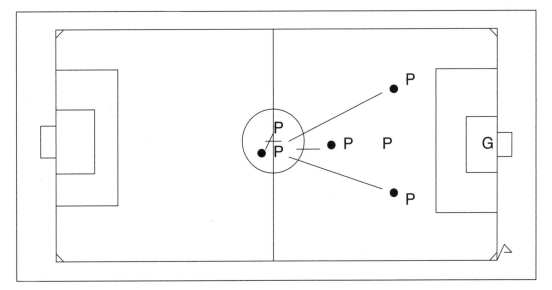

***Figure 17.8* Kickoff Formation, 6 or 7 Players**

the opponent's end. That way, your team maintains control of the ball, and they decide where they are going and what they are going to do.

In the formation in Figure 17.8 using six or seven players, the two players in the center circle start the play. One player will roll the ball forward, and the other player receives the ball and passes it back to one of the fullbacks. This gives your team time to move down the field. As the forwards and halfbacks move down the field, the fullbacks move down the field with the ball. As the opposing team rushes the ball, the ball can then be passed down the field to a player that is open. This enables your team to control the ball and set the tempo of the game. By passing the ball back, you maintain control, and that is what you want to do. If you are playing with six players, move the player just behind the center circle into the circle, and move the center fullback up closer to the center circle.

The formation in Figure 17.9 uses eight or nine players. The more players, the more options you have for kickoffs. As shown, after the original player rolls the ball, the second player can go to the players to their right or left, or she can go back. Normally the ball will go back, but if someone is on the wing and is not covered, it can be moved right or left.

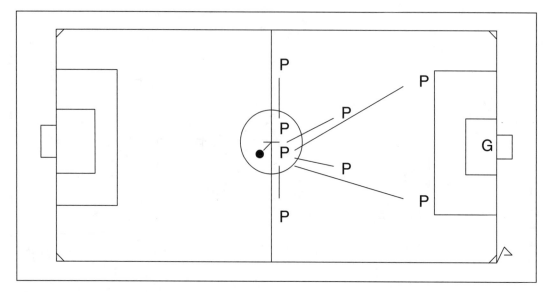

Figure 17.9 Kickoff Formation, 8 or 9 Players

Remember that passing the ball back to your fullbacks creates time to allow your up-front players to move into position. This spreads out the field and creates openings. If you are playing with eight players, move

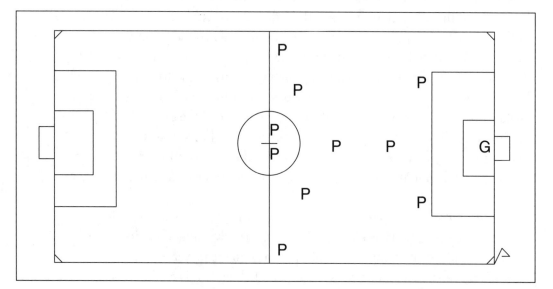

Figure 17.10 Kickoff Formation, 11 Players

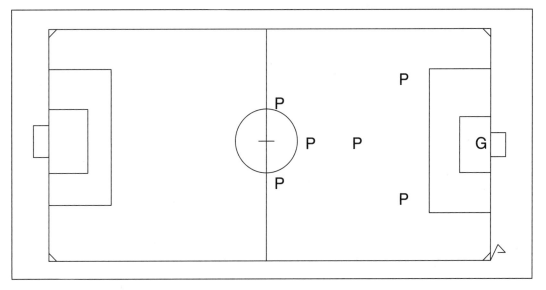

Figure 17.11 **Receiving Formation, 6 or 7 Players**

the center fullback behind the center circle, and let all other players remain in the same positions.

The formation using 11 players (Figure 17.10) gives numerous options for kickoffs. The ball can be moved to any of the players. There is another advantage: older players can pass the ball farther, and as such, the players can go from touchline to touchline. Have the players in the center circle pass the ball back to the defense, and allow the defense to move the ball forward or pass among them to move the ball. While they are doing this, the other players all get into position to score.

Receiving Formations

When you are in a receiving position, the object is to get the ball away from the opposing team as quickly as you can. With that in mind, you have to place players around the center circle to prevent the players from going forward and to also allow your team to quickly move to capture the ball. As soon as the other team rolls the ball, have your players move into the center circle. You must disrupt the other team's flow. By keeping your fullbacks near the penalty box, your team can also respond to

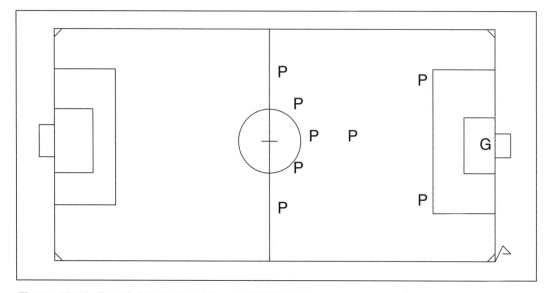

Figure 17.12 **Receiving Formation, 8 or 9 Players**

a team that just kicks the ball down the field. Remember that a goal can-not be scored on kickoff unless it is touched first by the opposing team.

In a formation using seven players (see Figure 17.11), you can put three around the center circle and still have all three fullbacks in posi-tion. If playing with six players, move the center fullback up to cover the center, leaving the other two fullbacks in a position to receive a hard kick. If the team is playing without a goalie (some younger teams do not have goalies), then you can either put the center fullback back or keep that person up near the center circle. If the kickoff team kicks it at the goal and it goes in untouched, it is not a goal. A goal cannot be scored by kickoff. If the ball is passed to a second player on the kickoff team and then kicked into the goal, it is a good goal. It will also be a goal if it hits a player on your team and then goes in. Any touch by a second player counts.

The object with eight or nine players (Figure 17.12) is the same: to prevent the opposing team from moving forward and to capture the ball as quickly as possible. Remember to move into the center circle as quickly as possible. With eight or nine players you can rush the three nearest the center circle and still have players to stop passes to the wing. If playing with eight players, just move the center fullback up to cover the very center of the circle.

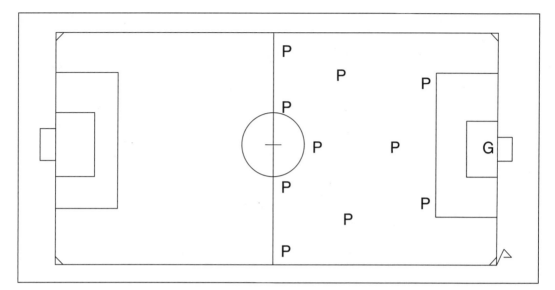

***Figure 17.13* Receiving Formation, 11 Players**

As you can see in Figure 17.13, using 11 players allows for perfect balance throughout the field. It is still important for the players to move forward quickly. The ones on the wings must move downfield to stop the passes and capture the ball. On older teams, it is doubtful you will ever see a team just kick the ball, but some have, just to throw the other team off. I feel it is best to keep control of the ball. With the 11-person formation, your team is ready to receive any type of kickoff.

18

Special Formations and Drills

There are a few different plays that require a specially designed formation. Your team will have to do the following:

- Goal kick
- Corner kick
- Direct kick
- Indirect kick
- Penalty kick
- Goalkeeper kick or throw

Having your team prepared to perform these actions and to defend these actions is important. It can often make the difference between winning and losing. It is necessary to run practice drills using the formations for offense and defense. These can be done when you are running centering drills, or support drills, or even kickoff and receiving drills. When the specific situation occurs, stop play and do the formation as a drill. If it doesn't work, stop play and repeat. Make sure that your players are in the correct positions and have the proper balance and support at all times.

Goal Kick

A goal kick is one of the most common kicks and is easy to execute. The goal kick is required when the ball rolls out of play, over the end line, and was last touched by the offensive team. To put the ball back into play (restart), it is placed in the goal box and kicked out of the penalty area. The opposing team's players cannot enter the penalty area or touch the ball until it has cleared the penalty box. The defending team (team kicking the ball) can be inside the penalty box, but they cannot touch the ball after the original kick until it clears the penalty box.

Kicking the Ball

Your team wants to get the ball out of their goal area without letting the opposing team have the opportunity to play the ball back into the goal area. The best way to do this is to kick the ball outside of the arc of concentration. When the ball is kicked straight out, it can easily be returned straight back in. The ball must be kicked to the corner/side area of the penalty box area. Your own team must be lined up in the penalty box area to keep the ball moving toward the opposite goal. That means you cannot put all of your players on the penalty box line. Some must remain downfield. There are 11 players shown in Figure 18.1. If you have fewer,

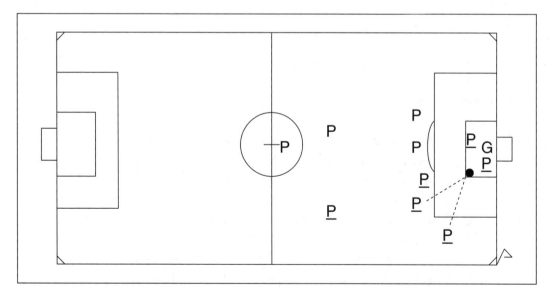

Figure 18.1 Goal Kick Formation

go with the underlined players and add as the numbers on the field increase. Emphasize to your team that if the ball cannot be passed, they should clear the ball as quickly as they can. The older players can easily put the ball out of the penalty area. The younger players (U-6 and U-8) will have some trouble getting it to the line. In the case of the younger players, it is not a time to dribble; they must clear the ball (pass/kick) out of the area. Even sending the ball out of bounds is better than losing it back into the penalty area.

Receiving a Goal Kick

When the opposing team is kicking the goal kick, you want to make sure your players are positioned to be able to return the ball back toward the goal as quickly as they can (see Figure 18.2). The kicking team will have fewer players in the goal area, and this is a great opportunity for your team to score. Many teams will kick the ball straight out until they learn that this is not the proper way to make a goal kick. Take advantage of the mistakes made by the other teams. Your team is there to capture the ball, so overload the line. With older teams, place your players on the line and also at the distance you estimate the team will be able to kick the ball. Cover the field (balance). Again, if you have a younger team

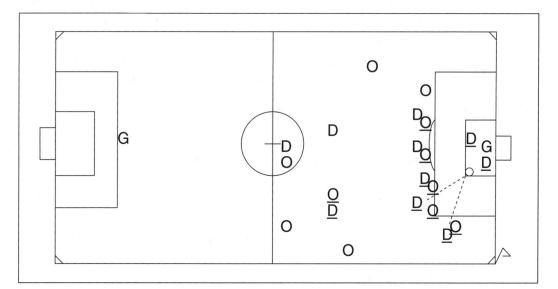

Figure 18.2 **Receiving a Goal Kick Formation**

with fewer players, place the underlined players first. Always keep the goalkeeper and at least one very good fullback downfield to stop any quick clearing of the ball. If the ball is kicked out, have your fullback send it right back (hard kick) into the penalty box area. If the fullback has time and is not being challenged by the opposing team, he can pass it to any open player on the team.

Corner Kick

A corner kick is not done often but may happen at least several times each game. A corner kick is required to restart play when the ball has rolled over the end line, out of play, and was last touched by the defensive team (team guarding the goal). Because the ball is placed in the corner (quarter) circle and kicked out, the ball is close to or on the end line, so being offside is not a problem on the kick. Follow-up kicks can result in being offside, especially if the defending team moves out into the field and the opposing players do not. You need to work with your team so they know how to execute the offense and defense.

Kicking the Corner Kick

The object of a corner kick is to get the ball into the goal area. There are two simple ways to do this. One is to kick the ball to a player standing close to the corner and have that person kick the ball into the goal. This play can result in an offside situation and can also be defended easily by the opposing team. The other is to kick the ball into the goal box area (see Figure 18.3). If the player is strong enough to kick the ball from the corner to the goal box, then your players have the option of using their head or feet to put the ball into the goal. As your players improve, they need to put spin on the ball so the ball is moving in the direction of the goal. A kick from the right-hand side (as you face the goal) is best done by using the left foot to place a clockwise spin on the ball. A kick from the left side is best done by using the right foot. This places a counterclockwise spin on the ball. With the ball spinning toward the goal, it will curl toward the goal and will maintain momentum because kicking the ball allows it to continue its movement toward the goal rather than having to stop its natural spin.

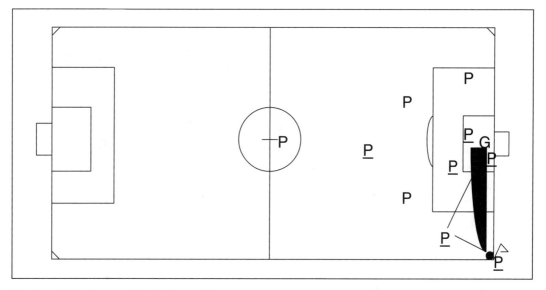

Figure 18.3 **Corner Kick Formation**

To put spin on the ball, have your player kick low on the ball and left or right of center, depending upon which spin you want. If the player is kicking from the right-hand side using her left foot, she will kick on the left-hand side of the ball, propelling her foot through the kick. If she is kicking on the left side, she will use her right foot and kick right of center on the ball. By leaning back when she kicks, she will cause the ball to rise. Balancing the body over the ball keeps the ball low and on the ground.

Defending the Corner Kick

Defending the corner kick is just a matter of covering all of the players on the opposing team. This is like man-to-man positioning. Your players must be in front of the other players to ensure they do not get the ball. You also need to post a player at the edge of the penalty box to stop any kick that is on the ground, going toward the goal. If any of your players get the ball, they need to clear the ball to the outside (outside the arc of concentration). They should try to put the ball into the area on Figure 18.4 that has hash marks. This is the safe area. Once the ball is cleared, your team can move to the ball in offense or regroup in for-

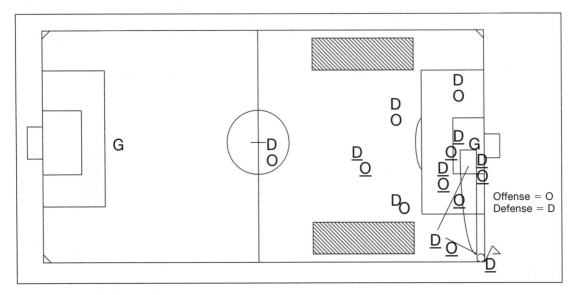

Offense = O
Defense = D

Figure 18.4 **Defending the Corner Kick Formation**

mation for defense. Again, if the ball is in the goal area, this is not a time to play with the ball by dribbling it out. Clear it and regroup.

Direct and Indirect Penalty Kick

A direct penalty kick is the result of a major foul committed outside of the penalty area. Direct means the ball can be kicked directly into the goal, without touching another player, and count as a score. The signal the referee gives to indicate a direct kick is with the arm straight out and pointing toward the goal. To defend against a direct kick, your players need to build a "wall," which is placing players together in a line blocking access to the goal (see Figure 18.5). To score a goal, you have to go through the wall or around the wall.

An indirect penalty kick is the result of a minor foul. Indirect means the ball has to take an indirect route to the goal. In other words, it must touch another player after the original kick, before it can go into the goal and count as a score. The signal the referee gives to indicate an indirect kick is to raise the arm into the air and point straight up. As in the direct kick, to defend against an indirect kick, your players need to build a "wall," which is placing players together in a line blocking access to the

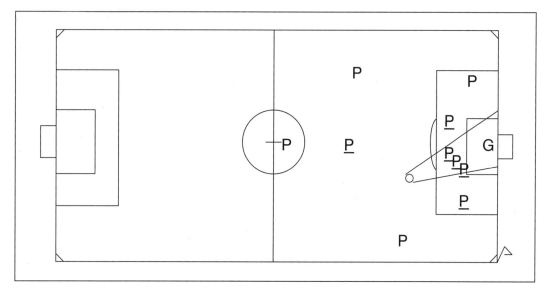

Figure 18.5 **Defending the Direct or Indirect Penalty Kick Formation**

goal. You also have to cover the other players because most of the time the ball will be passed. As you will see, there are different ways to accomplish the indirect kick and make it like a direct kick. To score a goal, you have to go through the wall or around the wall. Every situation is different, but with just a little practice, your team will be able to execute the defense against the direct and the indirect kick very well.

Defending Against a Direct or Indirect Penalty Kick

The best defense against a direct kick is to block access to the goal. This can be done by having your players create a "wall" to block the goal. The wall and any opposing player must be 10 yards from the ball. Quite often the players will form the wall closer than 10 yards. In this case the referee will ask them to back up or physically move them back to the 10 yards. Don't worry if your players are too close. Do worry if they are too far.

When the players are in the wall, there is always a possibility of a hand ball infraction (see Appendix) because often the ball is kicked directly into the wall. The natural defensive instinct by the players in the wall is to lift their hands to protect themselves. Have the boys place their arms down, with their hands together, covering their groin. This protects them and also keeps their hands occupied. Have girls fold their arms across their chests making an X with their arms. This keeps the ball from striking them in the chest; if their arms are hit but they did not move their arms, it is not considered an infraction.

The placement of the players in the wall is in a direct line across the face of the goal. If the ball is kicked at them, it is stopped; if it is kicked outside of them (left or right), it will travel wide of the goal. Because it is difficult for players to estimate their position when they are in the wall, you or the goalkeeper will have to direct their positioning. The best way to accomplish this is by having the end player in the wall face the goalkeeper. As the goalkeeper gives the directions, this person can move the line to comply. After the line or wall is established, the players turn back to face the ball. As with all balls inside the arc of concentration, players should clear it as quickly as possible.

Executing a Direct or Indirect Penalty Kick

To score on a direct or indirect kick, you must get the ball through the opposing team's players and past the goalkeeper. The chances of this happening are slight, but it does happen. That is why you must be prepared to attempt to score.

The best way to do this is to disrupt the other team's plans and position your own players where they can get the ball around the wall and into the goal. One way to disrupt the other team is to stick one of your players into their wall. When your player enters the wall, there will be pushing and shoving to get that player out. Make sure your player knows this will happen and keeps his cool. While the opposing team is worried about the person in the wall, they are not concentrating on the kick. The person in the wall can also be part of the play by kicking the ball directly at the player in the wall and having that player move out of the way to let the ball go through toward the goal.

Getting the ball around the wall requires your players to be positioned so they have a clear and open view of the goal. When the ball is passed to the player, that player must quickly kick it into the goal. This must be done before the goalkeeper can move into position and before the wall and the other opposing players can move to block the play. Figure 18.6 shows the ball being kicked directly into the wall at your own

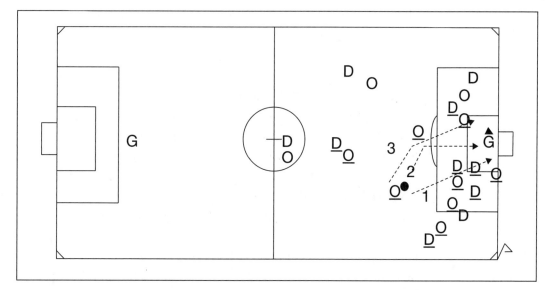

Figure 18.6 **Making the Direct or Indirect Kick**

player (1). In this case, you hope that the ball will ricochet off of one of the players and go into the goal before the goalkeeper can get it. The chances of this are very low. In a second case, the kicker passes the ball to the first player (2), who then passes it to another player (3) on the backside of the goal, and that person kicks the ball into the goal. Any time you can get the goalkeeper to move out of a set position, you have a chance of scoring. It is hard for the goalkeeper to gather or catch the ball when she is moving into a new position.

Penalty Kick

A penalty kick is a result of a major foul being committed by the defense while inside their own penalty area. The signal the referee gives to indicate a penalty kick is to hold the arm straight out and point to the penalty mark inside the penalty area. The kick is taken by placing the ball on the penalty mark. One player from the offense (team that was fouled) is allowed inside to kick the ball. The goalkeeper must stand on the line between the goalposts and cannot move until the ball is kicked. No other players from either team may enter the penalty area, including the penalty arc, until the ball has been kicked. If the ball is caught or blocked by the goalkeeper or if it bounces off the post, it is in play. Make sure the players move into the penalty area after the kick (see Figure 18.7). The chances of scoring on a penalty kick are high.

Taking the Penalty Kick

It is best if you, the coach, select the person to kick the penalty kick. Often the player that was fouled is still hurt and should not be allowed to kick. The kick does not have to be extremely hard, but it must be accurate. The kicker should pass the ball into the corner of the goal and never kick the ball directly at the goalkeeper. The best way to find out which of your players is the best at penalty kicks is to set up a goal using cones. Place cones on each side to be the goalposts, and then place a cone two to three feet inside each of these cones. Put the goalkeeper in between the inside two cones. Place the ball on the penalty mark, and have each of your players kick. The players that can consistently put the ball between the goal cone and the inside cone are your penalty kickers. Again, kicking hard is not as important as being accurate. Because the goalkeeper does not know where the ball is going to be kicked and cannot move until after the kick, the kicker has the advantage. Make sure your players move quickly into the penalty area after the kick in case there is a rebound and they may have another chance to score.

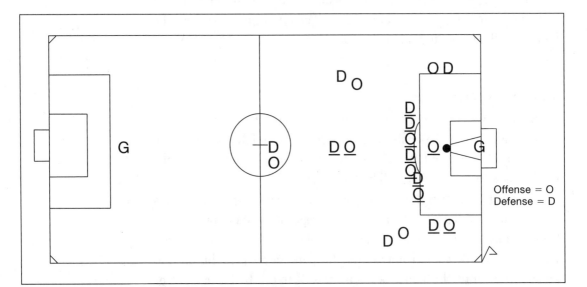

Figure 18.7 **Formation for the Penalty Kick**

Defending the Penalty Kick

There is very little defense against the penalty kick. If the kicker does not score, it is normally because he missed the goal completely. The goalkeeper will occasionally block a penalty kick, but that won't happen often. To prepare your goalkeeper for penalty kicks, make sure the goalkeeper watches the ball. The goalkeeper is given the time to set up in the goal; only when the goalkeeper tells the referee she is ready will the opposing team be allowed to kick. You can have your goalkeeper do one of two things to defend against the penalty kick. One is to just pick a side and dive in that direction when the ball is kicked. She has a 50-50 chance this way. The other possibility is to wait until the ball is kicked and then move in that direction. I prefer the second option, just in case the ball is kicked straight at the goalkeeper and can be blocked. Again, make sure your players are on the line and ready to go get the ball and clear it from the goal area if it is blocked or bounces off of the goalpost.

Goalkeeper Kick or Throw

When the goalkeeper makes a save and has the ball, he must put it back into play. The goalkeeper can either kick or throw the ball to his own teammates. Until the goalkeeper is strong enough to ensure the ball clears the penalty box, it is best to just get the ball outside of the arc of concentration.

Kicking or Throwing

When the goalkeeper gets the ball, she needs to slow down and let her own teammates move into position. Too often, the goalkeeper will get the ball and kick it as quickly as possible. That is not good. The goalkeeper needs to hold the ball and tell or motion to (or both) the players to move out to their positions. When they are in position, the goalkeeper can kick or throw the ball. The advantage of the kick is it normally goes much farther than a throw, but the disadvantage is that sometimes it is not very accurate. The advantage of a throw is that it can be very accurate for short distances. If the other team is not covering one of the fullbacks, the goalkeeper can throw the ball to that fullback, who can start moving the ball on offense. Remember that the goalkeeper can take

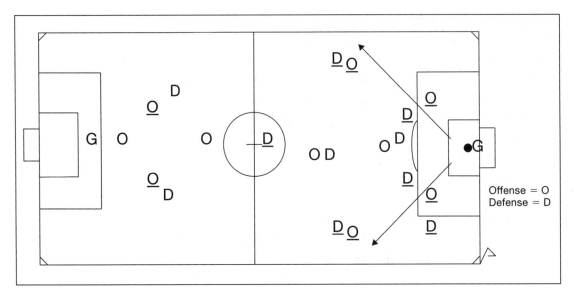

Figure 18.8 **Goalkeeper Kick and Throw**

Offense = O
Defense = D

three steps. She does not have to kick from where she stands. Have the goalkeeper take a few steps and then kick the ball. It enables her to get more power into the kick. By putting the ball to the outside of the field, as depicted by the solid arrows pointing away from the goal (see Figure 18.8), the goalkeeper keeps the opposing team from bringing the ball straight back to the goal. Even if the opposing team gets the ball, they are not in position to score.

Offense Against the Goalkeeper Kick or Throw

The best thing you can have your players do is to be ready for a bad kick. Have them on the penalty box line, with one player directly out from the goalkeeper, ready to return the ball into the goal. Many goalkeepers will make a bad kick or a kick down the center, which will allow your players to capture the ball while inside the arc of concentration. If the ball is to the outside, have your players take the ball toward the end line and center it into play. Again, balance is important. Players must be ready to get the ball and at the same time be ready to keep the opposing team from getting the ball.

Appendix

Glossary of Soccer Terms

All of the terms used in this glossary are defined related to how they apply to the game of soccer.

Advantage rule (law). A soccer law enabling a person or team to continue play after a foul was committed by the opposing team. The foul is not called if doing so would take the advantage away from the person or team in possession of the ball.

Alignment. How the players are arranged on the field. They must provide balance.

Arc of concentration. An area extending from the goalpost through the corner of the goal box and penalty area box and extending out to the touchline. This is the area where most goals are scored. The defense tries to keep the ball out of this area.

Assist. The action (usually a pass) that precedes the scoring of a goal. The player that assisted the player that scored.

Assistant referee (linesman/flagger). The person that assists the referee by controlling the touchline and looking for offside infractions. This person has a flag that is raised (and snapped, so as to be heard as well as seen) when an infraction occurs.

Attack. An attempt to score while having possession of the ball. This can be by person or team.

Attacker. Any player on the team that has possession of the ball.

Back. A defensive player.

Balance. How the team addresses the other team's players—in other words, how they play in relation to the person with the ball.

Ball. The soccer ball comes in three sizes: number 3, 4, and 5. Size of the ball used is dependent upon the age of the player. Official balls are white and black pentagon-shaped patches sewn together.

Beat. Getting past a player.

Bicycle kick. A specialty kick done by advanced players. The player brings the feet into the air and has both feet off the ground. The kick is made by bringing the feet forward, over the head, and striking the ball with the foot while the player is upside down and in the air.

Blind side. The area behind a player.

Bounce. When the ball hits the ground and rebounds back into the air.

Boundary lines. The lines on the field that mark the outer perimeter of the playing area. The boundary lines are a maximum of five inches wide.

Breakaway (break). When a player moves on goal undefended, creating a one-on-one situation with the goalkeeper.

Bylaws. The rules and regulations used by the soccer leagues to establish local policy.

Center. To kick the ball from the side of the field to the center of the field. This is done while in the vicinity of the opponent's goal. This gets the ball into the arc of concentration, which increases the scoring potential.

Center circle. The area in the center of the field used for starting play. This is done at the beginning of the game and at the beginning of the second half. It is also used to start play after a team scores. The opposing team cannot enter the center circle until the ball has been played by the kickoff team. The maximum size of the center circle is 10 yards from the center to the outside of the circle.

Center pass. Passing the ball from the outside to the center of the field.

Center spot. A mark (circle or X) in the center of the center circle. This is where the ball is placed for kickoffs to start or restart play.

Charge. Rushing a player and hitting the other player by using your body. This is a foul.

Chest trap. When the ball bounces off the chest and falls to the player's feet so that player can play the ball.

Chip. When the ball is kicked into the air as a pass or shot just hard enough to go over the head of the opponent.

Clear. Remove. To clear the ball means to get the ball and remove the ball from that area as quickly as possible.

Coach. The person in charge of training the players and conducting the players during games.

Cone. A plastic device that has a larger bottom than top and is used as an aid to mark specific areas. Often they are a bright color such as orange.

Corner arc. A quarter circle that is located on each corner of the field. The ball is placed in this area to restart play after the ball was kicked over the end line by the defending team.

Corner flag. A flag on a pole that is placed on the exact corner of the field to enable the players to see the maximum boundary of the field from a distance. It should be a minimum of five feet tall.

Corner kick. The method to restart play after the ball has crossed over the end line, going out of play, and was last touched by the defensive team

(team guarding the goal). The offensive team puts the ball into play by kicking it out of the quarter circle.

Cover. A defensive position where the player stays close to the opponent.

Cross. To send the ball from the outside of the field to directly in front of the goal.

Crossbar. The top post of the goal. It is always painted white.

Dangerous play. Any action on the field by a player, that could result in injury to another player.

Defender. The person that has the primary role of defending the goal.

Defense. The act of protecting the goal and preventing the opposing team from scoring.

Deflection. When the ball hits and bounces off of another player.

Depart. When a player leaves the field. No player may enter or depart the field without official referee permission.

Depth. The placement of players while in formation. Good depth is when the players are evenly dispersed from one end of the field to the other.

Depth (field). The length of the field from end line to end line.

Direct kick. The type of kick used after a major foul is committed. This is indicated by the referee pointing the arm directly toward the goal. The ball can be kicked directly to the goal. If the ball enters the goal, it counts as a score.

Draw. A game ending in a tied score.

Dribble. Moving the soccer ball, using your feet, while maintaining control of the ball.

Drills. The practice necessary to become skillful in soccer.

Drop ball. Used to restart the game. The referee drops the ball between two players. They cannot kick the ball until it has reached the ground.

Drop kick. When a goalkeeper drops the ball and kicks it after a bounce.

End line. The line at each end of the field. The boundary of the field length. It is also referred to as the goal line.

Enter. When a player comes onto the field. Must be during a restart (throw-in or goal kick) and must be with the permission of the referee. No player may enter or depart the field without official referee permission.

Equipment. The items needed by the coach or player to practice or play the game of soccer.

Far post. The goalpost that is the farthest from the ball.

Fast break. Advancing the ball down the field before the defense can respond.

Field. The area marked to enable teams to play the game of soccer. International games are played on fields 110 to 120 yards by 70 to 80 yards.

Field players. All players, except the goalkeeper.

Field the ball. To play the ball.

FIFA. Federation Internationale de Futbol Association. The official governing body for international soccer play and law.

Flagger (linesman/assistant referee). The person that assists the referee by controlling the touchline and looking for offside infractions. This person has a flag that is raised (and snapped to make a sound that the referee can hear) when an infraction occurs.

Flank. The outside of the field (wing) closest to the touchline.

Foot trap. Stopping the ball using your foot.

Formation. The placement of the players on the field. Formations are labeled by where players are positioned on the field. They are always counted starting with the fullbacks. The goalkeeper is not included in the count, and the count will never exceed a maximum of 10. For example, a 4-3-3 formation means 4 fullbacks, 3 midfielders, and 3 forwards for a total of 10 players.

Forward. The player that has the primary duty of scoring and in the formation is the closest to the opponent's goal.

Forward pass. Passing the ball down the field toward the opponent's goal.

Foul. An infraction of the rules. There are two types of fouls: major and minor.

Free kick. Any kick awarded to a team as the result of a foul.

Futbol. The official (and most-used) name for the game of soccer in every country except the United States and Canada.

Game clock. The official elapsed time of the game. The official time is kept by the referee.

Goal. The area at each end of the field that has a maximum width of eight yards, a maximum depth of six yards, and a maximum height of eight feet. The front edge of the goal is directly on the end line (goal line). The back of the goal is covered by a net to stop the ball when it enters the goal.

Goal box. The marked area directly in front of the goal. It is a maximum of 20 yards wide and 6 yards deep.

Goal kick. The method used to restart play after the ball has traveled over the end line, out of play, and was last touched by the offensive team (team trying to score). The defensive team places the ball in the goal box and kicks it out of the penalty box.

Goal line. The end line that marks the boundaries at each end of the field.

Goal scored. When the ball travels into the boundaries of the goal (must be completely over the goal line to be a goal). This means it is a score. Each score counts as one point.

Goal side. A term most commonly used by the defense, when their backs are to the goal. They want to keep themselves between the offensive player and the goal. The proper defensive position is facing the offensive player with the defensive player's back to the goal. They are said to be playing or staying goal side.

Goalkeeper (goalie). The player that stops the ball from traveling into the goal. This stop is called a save. The goalkeeper is able to use the hands while inside the penalty area. The goalkeeper must wear a different jersey to distinguish this player from the other players on the field.

Goalpost. The side bars on the goal. They are always painted white.

Half. The game is split into two halves of equal time. They are divided by a period called halftime.

Half line. The line that divides the field into two halves. The center circle is on this line.

Half volley. Kicking the ball after it has bounced on the ground but while it is in the air. This is done by having the upper leg and knee straight out from the body and striking the ball with the foot pointing straight down. This causes the ball to spin forward and curl down.

Halfbacks. The players that are in a position between the fullbacks and the forwards. They are also called midfielders.

Halftime. The period between the first half and the second half of the game. This period is used to allow the players to receive instructions, rest, and drink liquids. The halftime normally varies from 5 to 15 minutes, depending upon the age of the players.

Hand ball. An infraction caused by touching the ball with the hands or arms while it is in the field of play.

Hat trick. A minimum of three goals scored in one game by a single person.

Header. When the ball is played (moved or hit) by using the player's head.

Holding. Grabbing another player by the body or clothing, keeping that player from moving freely.

In bounds. When the ball is inside the boundaries of the field.

In play. When the ball is inside the boundaries of the field and is being played without being stopped by the referee.

Indirect kick. Used to denote the type of kick after a minor foul has been committed. This kick is denoted by the referee raising the arm straight up. The ball must take an indirect route to the goal. In other words, it must be touched by another player, after the original kick, before going into the goal.

Injury time. When a player is hurt, the game clock is stopped. Time is added to the game. This is at the discretion of the referee.

Instep. The portion of the foot where the soccer ball is passed. Normally this is on the inside of each foot.

Jersey (shirt). The garment worn by the player. Each team will have shirts that are different colors. The goalkeeper will wear a shirt that is different from the shirts of both teams on the field.

Juggling. The act of bouncing the ball using the feet, thighs, and head. The ball is moved from one point to the other while under control.

Keeper. A short name for the goalkeeper.

Kick. Striking the ball using the foot.

Kickoff. The method used to start a game or restart play after a goal.

Knock off the ball. A technique where the defensive player keeps his arms straight along his sides and uses pressure to move the offensive player off the ball. Elbows and arms that are sticking out, or pushes, cannot be used.

Laws. The rules that govern the play and conduct of the soccer game.

Linesman (flagger/assistant referee). The person that assists the referee by controlling the touchline and looking for offside infractions. This person has a flag that is raised (and snapped to make a sound that the referee can hear) when an infraction occurs.

Major foul. An infraction of the rules that is dangerous to the players on the field.

Manager. The person that assists the coach by making calls, doing paperwork, arranging rides for players, etc.

Marking. When a player is placed in a position to play one-on-one with an opposing player.

Match. The actual soccer game.

Midfielders. The players that are in a position between the fullbacks and the forwards. They are also called halfbacks.

Minor foul. An infraction of the rules that does not fall in the dangerous play category.

Near post. The goalpost closest to the ball.

Net. The covering on the back and sides of the goal. It can be seen through but will stop the ball when the ball enters the goal.

Nutmeg. A name used for the act of a player kicking the ball between the legs of an opposing player. This is usually embarrassing to the person that had the ball kicked through her legs.

Obstruction. When a player uses his body to get in the way of a person rather than playing the ball. This is a foul.

Offense. The act of moving the ball with the objective of scoring in the opposing team's goal.

Official. The referee and assistant referees that have responsibility for controlling and governing the game.

Offside. When an offensive player does not have one defender (and the goalkeeper) between her position and the goal, when the ball is kicked by her own teammate.

One touch. Striking the ball upon initial contact. Shooting or passing without dribbling.

Open space. Any area on the field where there is no other player.

Opponent. The team you are playing against.

Out of play. When the soccer ball or a person is outside the boundaries of the playing field.

Overlap. Running past another of your own teammates to advance down the field and get in position for a pass or shot.

Pass. Moving the soccer ball from one player to another.

Penalty arc. A portion of a circle on the outside center of the penalty area. It is not part of the penalty area, but players must stay outside this area when a penalty kick is being made. The players must maintain 10 yards from the kick. This line extends the penalty area line to ensure 10 yards of spacing.

Penalty area. The area in front of the goal that serves as the boundary for the goalie to be able to touch the soccer ball using his hands. The width is a maximum of 44 yards with a maximum depth of 18 yards.

Penalty kick. The method of kick used when a major foul is committed inside of the penalty area by the team defending the goal. The ball is placed on the penalty mark, and one player from the team fouled (offense) enters the penalty area to kick while only the goalkeeper from the defending team is allowed inside the goal area.

Penalty mark. A mark inside of the penalty area where the ball is placed for a free kick after a direct foul has been committed inside the penalty area. It is a maximum of 12 yards from the goal line, placed directly in the center of the goalposts.

Pitch. A British term used to denote the soccer playing field.

Play on. A term used by the referee to tell players to continue play. This is normally used in conjunction with the advantage rule.

Player. A person engaged in the game of soccer.

Point. The measure used to denote a goal scored. There is one point counted per goal scored.

Possession. When your team or player has the ball.

Practice. The time used to condition the players and teach the players the aspects of the game.

Quarter circle. The quarter circle mark that is on each corner of the field. The ball is placed in this area to restart play after the ball was kicked over the end line by the defending team.

Rainbow kick. A kick that is accomplished by putting the ball between the feet, using one foot to roll the ball up the back of the leg and the heel of the other foot to kick the ball over the player's head from behind. The ball travels from the rear of the player to the front, taking the arc made by a rainbow.

Receiving. The action of gathering or collecting the ball.

Red card. A card, colored red and about the size of a playing card, used by the referee to inform a player and team that the player is being ejected from the game. This player cannot be replaced by the team, and the team must play one person short. Two yellow cards for the same infraction of the rules equal a red card.

Referee. The person(s) on the field responsible for enforcing the laws of the game.

Restart. The term used to denote when the ball is put back into play after a stoppage of the game.

Rules and regulations. The bylaws used by soccer leagues to establish local policy.

Run. A move made by a player, without the ball, to get into another position.

Save. Any move made by the goalkeeper that stops the ball from going into the goal.

Score. The points earned by each team. Each goal counts as one point.

Shielding. Protecting the ball to keep from losing it to a player on the opposing team. This is done by placing the body between the opposing player and the ball.

Shin guards. The protective device worn under the socks to protect the players when they are kicked in the shins.

Shirt (jersey). The garment worn by the player. Each team will have shirts that are different colors. The goalkeeper will wear a shirt that is different from those of both teams on the field.

Shoes. Soccer shoes are designed to give the player traction and allow the player to kick and dribble without the shoe snagging on the ground. There is no cleat underneath the toe of the shoe. The cleats start on the sole of the shoe, at the toe, on the right and left sides.

Shorts. The short pants worn by soccer players. Colors can either match or contrast with the shirts worn by the players.

Shot. When the soccer ball is propelled toward the goal by the offensive team.

Shoulder charge. A legal play that allows a defender to press against the person with the ball. The defender's arm must be straight down along her side, and the pressure must be constant.

Skills. The actions required to perform the game of soccer.

Slide tackle. When a player slides or moves into the ball to take it away from the opponent.

Socks. Garments that cover the feet and the shin guards on the players. They are knee high. These can match or contrast with the uniform.

Square. Being directly to the right or left of the player with the ball.

Start. Denotes when the game begins in the first and second half.

Steal. To take the soccer ball away from an opponent.

Stopper. The defender that is in the front of the other defenders and closest to the centerline. Normally used to mark a player from the other team.

Strategy. The approach used to formulate the game plan.

Striker. The forward that is in the center position.

Substitution. Replacing one player on the field with another player that is off the field. This can be done only during certain restarts in the game and with referee approval.

Support. When players move into a position to assist and support the player with the ball.

Sweeper. The defender that is the last defender and plays in front of the goalkeeper.

Tackle. When a player slides into the ball to take it away from his opponent.

Techniques. The actions used to enable a player to understand and participate in the game.

Through pass. Passing the soccer ball so it goes beyond the defense into open space. This is used to put an offensive player behind the defensive player.

Throw-in. The method used to restart the game when the ball has traveled out of bounds over the touchline. It is thrown in by the team that did not cause it to go off the field.

Time-out. When the game clock (kept by the referee) is stopped. This can be called only by the referee and is normally used only for serious injuries.

Touch on ball. Denotes the proper foot movement and control on the ball.

Touchline. The line that runs on each side of the field. It is the boundary for the width of the field. It is also referred to as the sideline.

Trap. Stopping the ball to gain control. This can be done using the feet, chest, thighs, etc.

Tripping. A major, direct, foul.

Turnover. Losing the ball to the other team.

Under. Used in soccer to denote the age of the players. It is used in conjunction with a number. For example, U-6 means the players must be under the age of six.

Uniform. The shirt, shorts, and socks worn by the players that match those of their teammates (except the goalkeeper).

Victory. Winning the game.

Volley. Kicking the ball while the ball is still in the air. This is done by having the upper leg and knee straight out from the body and striking the ball with the foot pointing straight down. This causes the ball to spin forward and curl down.

Wall. A gathering of players, side by side, to block a kick from going through them to the goal, and instead making the kick go to their right or left.

Wall pass. A technique using two or more players to pass the ball around the opponent. Often referred to as a give-and-go.

Width. Coverage of players, while in formation, from side to side on the field. Good width is even spacing covering from touchline to touchline.

Width (field). The length of the field from touchline to touchline.

Wing. The outside of the field, closest to the touchline.

Winger. Normally refers to any forward that plays on the right- and left-hand side of the field. It can be used to describe any outside player.

Winning. Being the team that scores the most points.

World Cup. Soccer games played every four years by professional teams from all participating countries in the world. This is the largest sports event in the world and is controlled by FIFA.

Yellow card. A card, colored yellow and about the size of a playing card, used by the referee to warn a player and team that the player is being cautioned for an infraction of the rules. Two yellow cards for the same infraction in the same game are equal to a red card.

Zone play. When players are situated in a set area of the field that they must defend.

Index